THE STORY TEMPLATE

Conquer Writer's Block Using
the Universal Structure of Story

What Others are Saying...

Amy Deardon's *The Story Template* is a writer's conference in a single book. Building brick upon brick, she teaches the writer how to create his novel, from the basics of story structure, plot, and characterization, to writing a synopsis and publishing. I wish I'd had this detailed tool when I first started writing.

~VICKIE MCDONOUGH AWARD-WINNING AUTHOR
OF 23 BOOKS AND NOVELLAS

I love *The Story Template*'s clear language and story-building exercises. In my writing, I've never been successful with traditional outlines; *The Story Template* helps nail down plot points, yet doesn't suffocate the spontaneity that I love about the creative process. I work with teen writers, and this will be my go-to book for helping them construct a story.

~STEPHANIE MORRILL, AUTHOR OF *THE REINVENTION OF SKYLAR HOYT* SERIES AND CREATOR OF GOTEENWRITERS.COM

Amy makes me want to pick up the pen and launch into a new novel because she makes it sound so easy. A practical guide for fiction writers at any level, certain to unlock creativity because it takes care of the nuts and bolts of story construction, freeing the imagination to do its thing.

~GRACE BRIDGES, MANAGING EDITOR, SPLASHDOWN BOOKS

The Story Template contains a spiral of information, building upon itself in a way that works with my brain. Kudos to Amy Deardon for a simple, useful guide to story planning.

~VALERIE COMER, AUTHOR OF *TOPAZ TREASURE*

The Story Template is an amazing method for plotting a novel. Each step in the process is thoroughly evaluated and worked out in a series of exercises. Applying these exercises to a future project and a current one helped me prepare and assess them. I found tools to overcome my weak points in structure, and I look forward to the final results in my next writing project after implementing these exercises from start to finish. Thank you for letting me read this!

~Sarah Tipton, aspiring author

Amy Deardon's "template" is an excellent tool for the beginning writer, and a terrific method for organizing and brainstorming your story even if you're a seasoned professional. I utilized some of the template methodology for my current work in progress, and it works great!

~Kathy Harris, fiction author and non-fiction contributor to *Chicken Soup for the Soul: Thanks Mom*; *All My Bad Habits I learned from Grandpa*; and *The One Year Life Verse Devotional*

In *The Story Template*, Amy Deardon pens a thought-provoking guide to writing fiction adaptable for use by the novice as well as the multi-published author. The exercises she designs will enable all levels of writers to construct a more concise, exciting manuscript. I wish she had written this book sooner.

~Kassy Paris, co-author of *The Lazy M Ranch* series

The Story Template helped me see the big picture of my story. The book is full of tools to help the writer keep the story on track and strengthen the story lines to make the book a memorable read. I'm hoping that using *The Story Template* will take my novel from mediocre to memorable.

~Patricia Carroll, aspiring author

Amy Deardon has written a book that clearly demonstrates how to write a manuscript through a series of assignments that build on one another. It is thought provoking and logical. She includes a section on publishing and a very thorough segment on marketing and platform building. If you've ever said, "I should write a novel," this book is your place to start. Even if you are published, this is a good read.

~TOM BLUBAUGH, AUTHOR OF *NIGHT OF THE COSSACK* AND *THE GREAT ADVENTURE*

Nice addition to a writer's library, filling in the missing gap between screenplay and novel writing. A beginning writer could have a well-written book after following the included exercises.

~DIANA LESIRE BRANDMEYER, AUTHOR OF *WYOMING WEDDINGS*; *A BRIDE'S DILEMMA IN FRIENDSHIP, TENNESSEE*; AND *WE'RE NOT BLENDED, WE'RE PUREED: A SURVIVOR'S GUIDE*

Amy Deardon comes at the premise for this book from a writer's perspective as well as using the scientific method. Springboarding off Aristotle's famous three act structure made popular by many story and screenwriting texts, the author adds another dimension she refers to as the "template" for story—not a paint by numbers pattern, but a living, breathing structure common to all stories that gives them a life of their own.

I think this book will be helpful to writers both new and experienced. I plan to use it when I start on a new novel and also to re-work some novels that need a new chance at life! Excellent help for all levels.

~ROSE ALLEN MCCAULEY, AUTHOR OF "NICK'S CHRISTMAS CAROL" IN *CHRISTMAS BELLES OF GEORGIA*

THE STORY TEMPLATE

Conquer Writer's Block Using
the Universal Structure of Story

AMY DEARDON

Taegais Publishing

ISBN 13: 978-0-9818997-3-2
Library of Congress Control Number: 2011931881

Publisher's Cataloging-in-Publication data

Deardon, Amy.
    The story template : conquer writer's block using the universal structure of story.
    p. cm.
    Includes index.
    ISBN 978-0-9818997-3-2
1. Fiction --Authorship. 2. Fiction --Technique. 3. Plots (Drama, novel, etc.). 4. Motion picture authorship. 5. Motion picture plays --Technique. 6. Writer's block. I. Title.

PN3355 .D26 2011
808.3 –dc22   2011931881

Dedication

To You, the Writer

Table of Contents

Level Five: Integration

Level Six: Genesis

Level Seven: Refining

Introduction

Writing a novel or screenplay sounds like a great idea until you sit down to start. Where do you start? Many different methods exist to write the story, ranging from extensive pre-planning to venturing onto the first page without an idea. This book describes an approach to developing story—laid out as a sequential series of exercises to facilitate implementation—that you can use whether you prefer a structured or loose approach to writing. You can use it at the start to develop an idea fragment, or later to rescue a partial or completed manuscript that doesn't seem to be working. The method works whether you want to write plot-driven (genre) or character-driven (literary) stories. It enables you to efficiently use your time and creativity by breaking down the process of story building into a logical plan. You will not waste time sitting at your keyboard, wondering what you should write and how you can organize your ideas into a complete manuscript.

The idea for this book originated from my own learning process in producing a novel. Having written scientific articles, newspaper columns, and other nonfiction, when I decided to write a novel I was surprised by how difficult it was to get the words down. I tried outlining, and I tried just going ahead. I had wonderful ideas, but although the scenes I wrote were exciting the story itself often seemed somehow "wrong." I threw out more pages than I care to remember. Through sheer grit I finished the novel, but when I thought about writing another my heart sank. I decided to first solve the problem of understanding how story worked.

I chose twenty entertaining, modern novels in different genres, and fifteen more-or-less recent films (and I've since confirmed my preliminary observations with tens of more stories). One at a time, I took them apart: I made a list of each scene, then did a word count or timed the scene, calculated percentages and other statistics, and graphed each story onto a five page chart. I studied each story's progression, then compared the progressions of different stories to determine common pathways. I also read all that I could on constructing stories. The writing how-to literature was heavy on techniques (plotting, point of view, characterization, dialogue)—all of which are important—but there wasn't much on blending it all together. Screenwriting how-to books were stronger on structure, but still didn't give me all I needed.

I studied story after story, puzzling out how they were built. First, I identified elements called story posts, and found that these posts fell reliably within the timing of the whole. Then I found consistent trends of progression in the plot, as well as consistent trends of development and interactions in the characters. My biggest surprise, in fact, was finding just how unvarying were the underlying levels of the story. I also identified a unit of story construction I call a "bubble" that bridges the gap between the high concept ideas for the story and individual scenes.

Once I had my background knowledge, I coached students to develop their stories, and thereby constructed an algorithm for the practical application of this theory.

So, what is this "story template" that is the title of this book? Is this a formula or blueprint you can mindlessly follow, like a paint-by-numbers canvas?

In a word, no. I like to call what I found a template since it describes the shape or progression, on a deep level, of virtually all stories. Recognizing this pattern in a story is something I liken to sketching a face. An artist will tell you that a person's eyes are about halfway down the head, and are separated by another eye width. The bottom of the nose is halfway between the eyes and the chin, the mouth is proportionally between the nose and the chin and extends to imaginary vertical lines drawn below the eyes' pupils, the tips of the ears hit about eyelid level, earlobe tips at bottom-nose level, and on and on. Faces are infinitely varied, yet if the artist ignores these rough proportions, no matter how carefully sketched the face will always look "wrong." Similarly, you will use the template to ensure that your story elements are proportionally correct and all present. The template gives you a guide, but never dictates, what you can write.

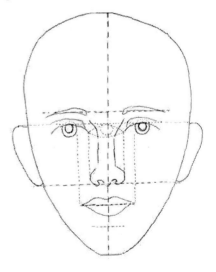

Getting the story shape right is the first, and (in my opinion) the hardest step to writing a gripping novel or screenplay. Without good structure, the story tends to meander without a point: although it may have high action, it is characterized by low tension.

You may want to first read this entire book to get an overview of story before starting with the exercises. Keep in mind that shaping a story is intensive work, and it will take you weeks or even months to get your story organized. This is normal. Don't get discouraged, and don't skimp on the exercises. Take your time to thoroughly work through each step. At the end, your story will be much stronger, and the actual writing will go like a dream.

This book is not sufficient for producing a finished story ready for publication or production. You will need to master further writing techniques such as characterization, description, dialogue, transitions, editing, etc. I will touch upon a few of these to give you some direction, but the only way to get really good is to practice. Fortunately, many excellent books are available for help. See Appendix One to start.

Outline of The Plan

I like to use the metaphor of constructing a house to envision building a story. To assemble a house, you move from larger to smaller elements to sequentially put something together. Only after you have worked through many tasks is it finally time to do the fine details of painting the windowsills and installing the wallpaper. Similarly, while you have ideas about character arcs and plot twists, and maybe you've even written some scenes, you will be well served to develop a direction before writing through your manuscript. If you write your first draft as the ideas occur to you, then this will comprise your story planning. You'll find that you probably don't have enough material to form an entire novel or screenplay, and even if you do it may not hang together. Believe me, this is a laborious and frustrating way to go.

The Story Template gives a series of actions for you to do that will allow you to develop your story ideas with a minimum of angst and wasted energy. Some exercises will be quick, others will require a great deal of thought, and perhaps even a marination of thought, before finishing. Don't be in a rush—some of your best ideas will come as you play with character or event possibilities. As you continue to develop your story you will probably revisit different components of these exercises, going back and changing previous work, as you move through this programmed story outliner. That's okay. Just go with the flow, and have fun.

When you've finished with these exercises, you will be ready to start writing your manuscript, with ease and flow and speed, because you will have already done the hard organizational work. Even if you want to change the story as you're writing, you'll be able to do so with an understanding of how to balance the changes. You will have a detailed roadmap that will allow you to bring your vision—your book or screenplay—to completion.

Writing Tools

You are a writer. Before you start, you need to assemble the following items:

1. A tool with which to do your major writing, either a computer, an old-fashioned typewriter, or paper and pencil. If you do handwrite your notes, you may want to treat yourself to a special pen that you love, and is only to be used for your *magnus opus*.

2. A system to organize your template exercises. I prefer hard copy: printing out computer files, or writing on loose leaf paper, then placing the sheets in a three-ringed binder. This notebook may inspire you and give you a sense of accomplishment as you look through to see how much you've done. Not as recommended is keeping files only on computer because they're harder to flip through, mark up, and juxtapose ideas; or a spiral or bound notebook because you can't replace pages or change their order. But do what works for you.

3. A small notebook to carry with you at all times. Use this to jot down any thoughts that come to you.

4. Index cards. Get two packs, and we'll go over how to use them to story board. Also get a roll of masking tape and a permanent marker (thin tip) for bold marks. Finally, you may want to purchase an index card binder to permanently keep your cards in order.

Getting the Words Down

Here are some tips to help you get the words down:

1. Decide on a daily quota of words that is manageable. A good starting goal might be 300, but remember to keep pushing this number up as you become accustomed to the writing process. Create a log to record your daily output. Post this on your refrigerator or otherwise keep it prominent in your daily life.

2. Set aside at least fifteen minutes at a time in which you can remain undisturbed. Aim for an hour or more if you can.

3. Don't start your writing session by checking your e-mail or doing anything else except for writing.

4. Turn off anything that might distract you—music, radio, or television. Some people can write through these things, but try without for a few days to see if you do better.

5. If you're stuck, do free-writing where you talk to yourself on paper. Something like, "I'm trying to figure out what Jason's problems with Mike might be in this scene. I was thinking about…"

Let's get started.

LEVEL ONE:

Beginning Thoughts

You are now on the first level of story construction. On this level you're going to scout out your preliminary ideas to determine what sort of story you want to write and how you might go about doing this. If you have a stalled piece of writing, or a completed-but-not-working manuscript, make sure you still do this level's exercises: you may be surprised by the hidden connections and ideas you find.

Chapter One

Four Story Pillars and One Logline

What are you going to write about? You may have a striking image, or a character, or a situation, for which you feel compelled to write something. You may even be fortunate enough to have already written some pages. This level will help you start to organize your ideas.

A technique called free-writing will be essential to you as you go through these exercises. Basically, you talk to yourself as you record your thoughts on the computer screen or paper as they occur. Don't self-edit or otherwise worry about what you're putting down. If you don't know what to say next, write "I don't know what to say next because..." and go from there. The thought is that if you're not worried about exactly how you write something, the ideas will come more freely. And don't worry about the chaos—no one is going to see your exercises except you.

At the end of each exercise, write a cogent summary of your answer.

Remember that, at this point, everything is fluid. Don't be afraid to make decisions because they are easy to change. Just put something down.

Ready? Let's go.

Exercise 1: Similar Stories

List some stories from childhood that you loved. Why did you love them? What sorts of stories do you now read and/or go to the theater to see? What is it that attracts you to them?

As you envision your novel or screenplay name three or so stories that might be similar. If you can, take these books or films off the shelf to quickly review them. What do you like about them: interesting characters, exciting plot, a unique vision of the world? What sorts of story questions are raised? How might your story be similar, and different, to these stories?

Exercise 2: Current Status of Your Story

Write down the current status of your novel or screenplay. Why do you want to create it? How much have you already written, if any? Did you stop, and if so, why? If you have a vivid character or situation as the seed of the idea, put that down. What will happen in your story? Quickly list possible ideas, characters, scenes, or actions you might want to include.

The Four Story Pillars

A story is usually thought of as having two arms: an outer narrative and an inner one. The outer narrative covers the external plot: what your friend will summarize when you ask him what a movie or book is about. In contrast, the inner narrative describes an emotional journey and changes within the characters. Different types or genres of stories tend to emphasize different arms—for example, a romance or literary work focuses on inner story while a mystery or action-adventure emphasizes outer story.

A story can also be thought of as having two tiers of construction: concrete and abstract. The concrete tier describes the actual events and characters in the story, whereas the abstract tier comments on the broader applications of your story: why it may reflect society, relationships, or life.

I like to think of the story, then, as having four story pillars:

	OUTER STORY	INNER STORY
CONCRETE	Plot	Character
ABSTRACT	Story World	Moral

The fundamental concept that drives the story, or the story premise, comes from just one of these four areas. For example:

Plot – *Iron Man, Jaws*
Character – *Forrest Gump, Rocky*
Moral – *Facing the Giants, Ender's Game*
Story World – *Fellowship of the Ring, Harry Potter*

Plot is the most commonly used story pillar for the story premise.

It's possible to tell a story based mainly on the external pillars of plot and story world. For example, some hard-core adventure stories and Agatha Christie mysteries are plot-based and fun to experience—but the story evaporates as soon as it's finished.

A story becomes resonant as the internal pillars of character and moral are developed. In addition to an exciting journey, your reader or viewer is looking for an emotional experience and the ability to conclude something about life in general. If you wish your story to be something that people will want to experience over and over, you'll need to strengthen and coordinate each of these four pillars.

This level begins to explore these areas. In Level Two you'll develop each of these story pillars in detail.

Exercise 3: Premise Preference

Based on your answers to Exercises 1 and 2, write down this sentence:

For the story I'm writing, my premise will be THIS (Plot, Character, Moral, Story World).

If you're not sure, just go with one. This decision is not irrevocable.

Now, rank your second, third, and fourth preferred areas.

Exercise 4: Plot

Often at this stage you'll have in mind only a plot twist or other brief flash. Not to worry: write down as much as you have. Then brainstorm a little: what might be the ultimate outcome of this situation? What could launch a character to get into this situation in the first place? What might be the ultimate goal being pursued? What might be the main problem(s) to achieving this goal?

Exercise 5: Character

Who are some of the people you'd like to tell your story? Do you have one quirky or troubled personality, or maybe two or more characters who have strained relationships? Are your characters male or female, old or young? Do they have interesting jobs or backgrounds? What makes them unique? Also, plot often suggests certain types of characters. For example, a story about a new invention might need an inventor and/or a thief. A romance requires a man, a woman, and probably a rival. Write down a few ideas for characters.

Exercise 6: Moral

What is the main message you want your reader or viewer to learn from your story? It can be something like "Beware evil masquerading as good," or even "Bad guys get their comeuppance." Write down some ideas for your moral.

Exercise 7: Story World

Describe the primary environment(s) in which your story will take place. Put in anything that occurs to you—time and date, social customs, buildings, transportation, food, clothing, technology, etc. Does this world remind you of anything?

Exercise 8: Interlinking Areas

Look at your thoughts for the four story pillars in Exercises 4 through 7. Is there anything you can do to reinforce ideas between them? For example, how might constant rain in the story world reflect a theme of sorrow? How might a plot of a disappearing treasure be contrasted by a stand-out character? Go through your exercises and think about any parallels or contrasts you might be able to draw, then write them down.

Exercise 9: Preliminary Shape

Your ideas right now may be breathtaking, but in order for anyone else to understand you must be able to clearly communicate them. Now that you've thought a little about the components that might be in your story, take time to consolidate them.

For this exercise, talk to yourself on paper (or computer screen) about exactly who and what your story is about.

Is it primarily a romance or an adventure flick? Are there any important lessons learned? Does it end happily? Your writing may be fragmented and take three or more pages, but don't worry about putting down a lot of mush. You're clarifying your thoughts.

At the end, summarize your story in a few coherent sentences.

Logline

A logline is one sentence of about fifteen to twenty words that describes your story. There are many ways to write this logline. This formula produces good results if you're having trouble framing your sentence:

An (optional adjective) subject, in this situation, acts to do this.

Some examples:

The Wizard of Oz: A farm girl is transported to a magical land and must find her way home. (fifteen words)

The Fellowship of the Ring: A hobbit must destroy a magical ring of power before it destroys his world. (fourteen words)

Romeo and Juliet: Two teenagers from warring families fall in love and must overcome family obstacles of hate to stay together. (eighteen words)

The Count of Monte Cristo: A wrongfully imprisoned young man gains freedom and a fortune that he uses to wreak an elaborate revenge. (eighteen words)

The logline strips your story to its bare minimum. You'll notice that character names aren't used, yet the premise is specifically described. The logline doesn't have to follow this formula, but should contain irony if possible, and cause the listener to become intrigued. This is a deceptively challenging assignment: don't be satisfied with your first attempt. You'll return to writing the logline as you go further through the template, but start work on it now.

Exercise 10: One Sentence Story Description or Logline

Write your preliminary logline.

LEVEL TWO:

Building a Foundation

You are now on the second level of story construction. On this level you're going to establish a strong foundation for your story by constructing and integrating the four story pillars. When you've finished this level you'll have established the boundaries of your story so that you can imagine the rough outlines of what it will look like from beginning to end.

Chapter Two

Story World Pillar and Moral Story Pillar

The story pillars—plot, character, moral, and story world—form the foundation of your story. The best way to develop these is to start in, then keep circling through them a few times until they're deeply interconnected. This chapter will review the abstract pillars (story world and moral), and the next two chapters the concrete pillars (character and plot). You may wish to go over this chapter and the next two a few times until your pillars seamlessly interlink.

Story World Pillar

	OUTER STORY	INNER STORY
CONCRETE	Plot	Character
ABSTRACT	**STORY WORLD**	Moral

The story world is usually the easiest pillar with which to start. Remember that your story does not take place in a vacuum.

Some stories, especially in genres like science fiction, fantasy, and adventure, emphasize technology and special environments, but all stories must take place somewhere even if it's just around the corner.

Your story world should give just that sense: a world that is going on around your particular narrative. The reader or viewer wants to feel that there are many stories that could be told here, and they happen to be reading this one. Your world should seem large, and real, and immediate. You do this by using specific details to describe a specific place and environment.

If you are inventing a magical world, remember to put limits on any special abilities, talents, or phenomena so the reader or viewer perceives them as real rather than magically made-up. Think Superman with the kryptonite.

The story world can be developed to impinge upon the plot, to become almost another character, and/or to be a metaphor for the story moral. It serves as a reflection of ideas and themes, comparisons or contrasts, within your story.

The story world becomes compelling when you describe not just the environment, but your characters' reactions to it.

A word of caution: similar to character, some writers become obsessive about building their story world. By all means take time to understand the background, but remember that this *is* background. When it's time to write your story, you will need to include much less than you might think—just enough to give a tang.

Exercise 11: Story World

Describe the environment(s) in which your story will take place. Some ways to describe your story world include the time and date, social customs, languages, technology, buildings and structures, transportation, food and clothing, weather, and anything else you might think of. What do your characters think and feel about, and how do they respond to, this story world? When you're finished free-writing, write a succinct paragraph or two describing your story world.

Moral Story Pillar

	OUTER STORY	INNER STORY
CONCRETE	Plot	Character
ABSTRACT	Story World	**MORAL**

To write an emotional story you need to articulate one, and only one, universal principle or theme. This is the element that causes the reader or viewer to return again and again; it's the element that resonates deep within him. Yes, you can write a story without a moral, but if you do this the story will disappear as soon as the reader puts it down. A clever adventure or mystery is fun to experience, but without a moral it doesn't resonate.

The moral is the backbone of your story. You can bend or adjust the other story elements to fit the moral more easily than you can adjust or add a moral once you've planned the other parts.

I want to add a cautionary word here: stories resonate within us because they touch the emotions, and thereby open the mind to accept an illustrated concept. You need to be responsible when writing since the emotional draw of your story can lead someone to accept a bad premise. Your moral should be something true, and something edifying.

You should be able to express your story's moral in a single sentence. Here are some examples:

Romeo and Juliet: Great Love Defies Death.

Forrest Gump: Unconditional Love Redeems the Rebel.

Fellowship of the Ring: Willingness to Relinquish Absolute Power Leads to Preservation.

The Godfather: Family Ties Overcome Individual Virtue.

Rocky: Courage and Persistence Lead to Significance.

The Incredibles: Working Together Allows Each Individual to Shine.

How do you write your moral? One way is to use this process:

1. Identify the primary emotion or principle driving the story.
2. Refine this emotion so it's specific.
3. Determine what that emotion's opposite might be.
4. Imagine what the outcome will be when these two forces go head to head.
5. Write out the heart of your story in a single sentence.

Let's go through these.

Identify the Primary Emotion

You need to determine the overall theme or emotion you want to explore in your story. Some examples might be love, hate, forgiveness, anger, generosity, greed, humility, arrogance, friendship, enmity, courage, fear, truth, doubt, etc.

The Wizard of Oz: Longing.

The Fellowship of the Ring: Power.

Romeo and Juliet: Love.

The Count of Monte Cristo: Revenge.

Exercise 12: Moral Primary Emotion

What is the primary emotion you might wish to use to drive your story? Write down several alternatives, then choose one to go with.

Refine the Emotion

Can you further refine this emotion and make it specific? For example, if your primary emotion is love, then it could be the love of a parent for a child (or vice versa), love for animals, or love that fails.

> *The Wizard of Oz*: Longing for something outside of self.
> *The Fellowship of the Ring*: Absolute power.
> *Romeo and Juliet:* Great love between lovers.
> *The Count of Monte Cristo:* Righteous revenge against a great wrong.

> ### Exercise 13: Moral Refining the Primary Emotion
> *Think about the primary emotion driving your story. How can you focus it? Take some time to ponder, then write down your driving emotion in a succinct phrase.*

Determine the Emotion's Opposite

What is the opposite of the driving story emotion about which you will be writing? This opposite, or a powerful oppositional force, allows you to showcase the emotion.

> *The Wizard of Oz*: Longing for something outside of the self is opposed by something within the self.
> *The Fellowship of the Ring*: Absolute power is opposed by willingness to relinquish absolute power.
> *Romeo and Juliet:* Great love between lovers is opposed by death.
> *The Count of Monte Cristo:* Righteous revenge against a great wrong is opposed by failure of ability to carry out suitable punishment.

Exercise 14: Moral Opposite of Primary Emotion

Take some time to determine how your primary emotion will be opposed. This should be a strong oppositional force that will demonstrate just how powerful is your primary emotion.

Outcome when these Two Forces Go Head to Head

What happens when these two forces go head to head? Keep in mind that for most stories the positive will win over the negative.

> *The Wizard of Oz*: Longing for something outside of the self leads to the realization that the answer has been within the self all along.
>
> *The Fellowship of the Ring*: Willingness to relinquish absolute power leads to preservation.

NOTE: This is the protagonist Frodo's description of moral, since his is the main story. *The Lord of the Rings* trilogy also contains a subplot with Aragorn, the rightful king of Gondor, who is afraid to rule because he doesn't trust himself with power. Aragorn is an example of a technique called "protagonist's mirror" that I will discuss shortly. A description of Aragorn's moral might be: Courage to rightfully rule leads to healing. This subplot moral is a variant theme on the primary story emotion of power, and contrasts with the main story message. Using a contrasting subplot is a powerful method to deepen and discuss a story moral.

> *Romeo and Juliet:* Great love defies death.
>
> *The Count of Monte Cristo:* Righteous revenge against a great wrong drives carrying out suitable punishment.

NOTE: The end of this story demonstrates the importance of mercy and forgiveness, so a later description of the moral might be: Forgiveness mixed with righteous revenge leads to peace with oneself. This change in moral occurs when the author demonstrates the negative as well as positive results of the moral, then concludes with a different, related, moral. This technique deepens the author's discussion of ideas within the context of the story. Another example of a story using this technique is Orson Scott Card's *Ender's Game*.

Exercise 15: Final Moral of the Story

Free-write to determine the moral of your story. Can you think of ways to deepen your moral, either through different characters taking different parts of an argument, or one or more characters realizing that the end result of the original moral is futile or at least partially negative? Take some time to free-write your ideas. At the end, write your story moral and contrasting morals if present in a single phrase each.

Chapter Three

Plot Story Pillar

	OUTER STORY	INNER STORY
CONCRETE	**PLOT**	Character
ABSTRACT	Story World	Moral

The plot pillar describes the outward shape of your story. This is what people usually think of for a story, and what they will describe to you when you ask what a book or film is about. Interestingly, I found through my studies that the plot is the most stereotyped and predictable part of the story—although individual events can be original and stunning, the plot's overall shape is quite reliable. It is the writer's imagination and execution for situations of conflict, for characters, and for story world and moral, that makes a story unique and memorable.

Like it or not, aware of it or not, any plot that diverges too far from the structure I outline throughout this book will not seem avant-garde, but wrong. By being aware of plot elements and proportions, you can make sure that your story is consistent, complete, and satisfying.

Story Goal and Story Question

The story goal is the task that your protagonist wants to accomplish during the course of your story. This task needs to be something unequivocal, something that clearly is successful, or not, by the end of the story. Attaining this goal becomes the story question.

Here are some examples:

In *The Wizard of Oz*, the story goal is that Dorothy longs to return home. Failure occurs if she is unable to return home. The story question is: Will Dorothy be able to return home?

In *The Fellowship of the Ring*, the story goal is that Frodo must destroy the One Ring. Failure occurs if the ring is not destroyed. The story question is: Will Frodo be able to destroy the One Ring?

In *Romeo and Juliet*, the story goal is that Romeo and Juliet want to run away, be married, and live peacefully together in love. Failure occurs if they are not able to escape. The story question is: Will Romeo and Juliet be able to escape?

In *The Count of Monte Cristo*, Edmond is falsely imprisoned, then escapes and gains an enormous fortune. The story goal is that he wishes to take revenge on those who stole his youth, his career, and his fiancée from him. Failure occurs if the wrong doers get away with a great evil. The story question is: Will Edmond be able to suitably punish the guilty (without losing his integrity)?

Exercise 16: Story Goal and Story Question

Using the previous examples as a guide, free-write about possibilities for your story goal and story question. Make the goal specific and unequivocal. At the end, summarize the story goal and story question in one sentence each.

Stakes

You also need to decide why this story goal is so important to your protagonist. If it isn't important, he won't be motivated to achieve it. What horrible things might happen if the story goal isn't achieved?

Here are some examples:

In *The Wizard of Oz*, if Dorothy fails to return home, she will be stuck forever in the strange landscape of Oz, never again seeing her family.

In *The Fellowship of the Ring*, if Frodo fails to destroy the One Ring, Middle Earth will fall into chaos and horror under Sauron's dominion.

In *Romeo and Juliet*, if Romeo and Juliet fail to escape, Juliet will be forced to marry against her will. She and Romeo will never see each other again.

In *The Count of Monte Cristo*, if Edmond cannot wreak an appropriate revenge, great evil will go unpunished.

Exercise 17: Stakes

Free-write to discover why the story goal is so important to your protagonist. What horrible consequences will occur if your protagonist fails in his quest? Often the stakes escalate throughout a story, so you should think of several levels of jeopardy. Also, there may be multiple bad emotional and physical consequences, and others affected besides the protagonist. At the end, summarize your stakes in a sentence or two.

Obstacles

If your protagonist can simply go and achieve the story goal, there is no story. All stories need multiple obstacles, both internal and external, holding the protagonist back from getting what he wants. An important rule for writing is to never make it easy on your hero.

Here are some examples:

In *The Wizard of Oz*, Dorothy is a farm girl whose dog is stolen, then within a tornado she is transported to a strange and magical land. She doesn't know how she's going to find the wizard of Oz and must battle various creatures and situations, including multiple run-ins with the wicked witch of the West. She also has to figure out how to get the wizard of Oz to help her. Internally she's plagued by uncertainty and insecurity.

In *The Fellowship of the Ring* Frodo must make his way past the Nazgûl to fight Orcs, rough terrain, Gollum, and other varied creatures and problems. Internally he finds carrying the Ring of Power an almost unbearable emotional burden.

In *Romeo and Juliet*, the Montagues and Capulets are at war. Friar John marries Romeo and Juliet, a deep secret that must be covered. Juliet's cousin Tybalt kills Romeo's best friend Mercutio, so Romeo kills Tybalt for revenge and must go into hiding. Friar John gives Juliet the potion so that she appears dead, thereby initiating the whole sequence of both Romeo and Juliet individually killing themselves for the other. Additionally, there are a number of internal obstacles, including Romeo's impetuous nature, Juliet's reluctance to marry Paris, and Juliet's nurse who gives her advice she doesn't want to hear.

In *The Count of Monte Cristo*, Edmond must learn to live alone in prison, then to escape, then to find the men responsible to wreak his revenge. His revenges are elaborate and full of twists. Internally Edmond copes with rage, power, and losing and gaining love.

Exercise 18: Obstacles

Come up with some internal and external obstacles that may occur in your story.

Simple Story

A story can be divided into three parts: beginning, middle, and end.

The beginning sets up the story, depicting the protagonist in his ordinary world and how and why he makes the decision to pursue the story goal. The middle, the longest section, consists of a series of actions and reactions that show the progress and problems of the protagonist pursuing the story goal. The end describes how the story is resolved.

Exercise 19: Simple Story

Determine where your protagonist starts, and where he will finish. Then identify in a few sentences what happens to your protagonist in the beginning, middle, and end of your story.

Preliminary Structure

Now you can start a preliminary structure of your story. A rough structure can be described using the story goal and six general points of the story flow:

Beginning
Bridging Story Goal
Door
Story Goal
Journey
Slide
Resolution

Beginning: Describes protagonist's ordinary world plus a change.
Bridging Story Goal: A goal that moves the protagonist to take action.

Door: The protagonist embarks on a journey to achieve the story goal.

Story Goal: Overall goal that the protagonist wants to achieve by the end of the story.

Journey: Long middle section of the story.

Slide: The action changes again, and the story moves onto a course of resolution.

Resolution: The end of the story.

Here are some examples:

The Wizard of Oz:

Beginning: Dorothy is a farm girl in Kansas when her dog Toto is taken from her by Miss Gulch.

Bridging Story Goal: She decides to get Toto back.

Door: A tornado lifts Dorothy and Toto into the Land of Oz.

Story Goal: Dorothy wants to convince the wizard of Oz in the Emerald City to bring her home.

Journey: Dorothy meets friends, and they have many adventures and trials traveling toward the Emerald City.

Slide: Dorothy kills the witch so that she can bring the witch's broomstick to the wizard, then he will help her go home.

Resolution: Dorothy learns the wizard is a fraud, but she uses the ruby slippers she's already wearing to get home.

The Fellowship of the Ring:

Beginning: Frodo lives in the Shire when he is given the One Ring by his Uncle Bilbo. Frodo wants to hide the Ring.

Story Goal: Gandalf tells Frodo the Ring must be destroyed in the fires of Mount Doom.

Door: Frodo leaves the Shire with Sam.

Journey: Frodo and Sam meet friends and form the Fellowship of the Ring. They have many adventures and trials traveling toward Mount Doom.

Slide: Orcs fall upon the group, and Frodo and Sam are separated from the others.

Resolution: The story is continued in the next two books/films, but in this one Frodo and Sam continue alone. Frodo realizes that only he is able to bear the Ring long enough to destroy it.

Romeo and Juliet:

Beginning: The Montagues and Capulets are at war. Romeo is in love with Rosaline. Although they are Montagues, Romeo and Benvolio decide to attend the Capulet party.

Bridging Story Goal: Romeo wishes to catch a glimpse of Rosaline at the Capulet party.

Door: Romeo and Juliet see each other at the party and fall in love, then learn their families are mortal enemies.

Story Goal: Romeo and Juliet want to live together in love.

Journey: Romeo and Juliet meet friends, and they have many adventures and trials traveling toward a life together.

Slide: Juliet drinks the potion that makes her appear dead.

Resolution: Romeo misses Father John's letter. He thinks Juliet is dead and kills himself, then she kills herself.

The Count of Monte Cristo:

Beginning: Edmond Dantès is a young sailor who has just accepted a captaincy, and is about to be married. He is thrown into jail under false charges as a political prisoner.

Bridging Story Goal: Edmond wants to escape prison.

Door: Edmond escapes and gains an enormous fortune.

Story Goal: Edmond wants to punish the great evil that caused him to lose his youth, his fiancée, and his life.

Journey: Edmond becomes many different persons, and has many adventures and trials as he enacts his revenge.

Slide: Edmond realizes that revenge must be tempered by mercy.

Resolution: Edmond forgives the last of his enemies, saves his friend's son, and sails away with a new love.

Exercise 20: Preliminary Story

Using the above examples as a guide, free-write ideas for each of your seven story points: Beginning, Bridging Story Goal, Door, Story Goal, Journey, Slide, and Resolution. Then write a summary sentence for each point.

Exercise 21: Putting the Preliminaries Together

Aim to write between a paragraph and half a page for what happens in each of the following events: Beginning, Bridging Story Goal, Door, Story Goal, Journey, Slide, and Resolution.

For the journey, identify at least four obstacles (internal or external) that your protagonist will encounter during his "many adventures and trials."

Exercise 22: One Sentence Logline

Review your logline (Exercise 10) and modify as appropriate. Use powerful verbs and nouns.

Conclusion

That was tough! Hopefully, you now have a clearer idea of the flow of your story and how it will be comprised.

Chapter Four

Character Story Pillar

	OUTER STORY	INNER STORY
CONCRETE	Plot	**CHARACTER**
ABSTRACT	Story World	Moral

The quirky, unique people of a story are what touch the emotions and make the story gripping for the reader or viewer. Who can forget Scarlett O'Hara, Sherlock Holmes, or Indiana Jones?

Writers use many techniques to develop a character, and you've probably heard of at least a few of these. For example, some writers spend hours working on character questionnaires describing physical characteristics, personality and mannerisms, personal and professional histories, and other information. Writers can develop interrelated character histories, family trees, and bombshell generational secrets. Others might keep a journal in the character's voice, or conduct in-depth interviews by pretending the character is sitting across the table. Some use a Myers-Briggs or other type of personality analysis. These are all fine, and you should feel free to use any techniques that help you to envision your story people. However, in my opinion the character arc is what makes or breaks the character. This is what I will focus on for the story template.

Let's go.

Developing the Protagonist

While you may have complex story ideas, it's important to identify one, and only one, protagonist for your story. The technical definition of the protagonist is that he is the character who most emotionally changes in the story: he learns how to repair an emotional void or need in his life so that he can live more freely. This character change, or arc, describes a journey of fulfillment.

Exercise 23: Who is Your Protagonist?

You need to decide whose story this will be. List all the characters you may want to include in your story, and describe your thoughts around them. How will each change, or will he change? Then look through your list to decide on which character you most want to focus. If there are two (or more) characters that make major changes, that's okay, but one has to be dominant. Make a choice.

Write down this sentence: My protagonist will be NAME.

Hidden Need

For a character arc, your protagonist must have a hidden need, which is an emotional lack that he must fulfill in order for him to be truly free. He discovers this fulfillment along his story's journey. The protagonist doesn't know what this lack is although he feels he is missing something. For example, Mitch McDeere in the film *The Firm* has just graduated at the top of his law class and has a lucrative job at a prosperous law firm, yet he must learn not to take the morally easy route for a tangible goal. Edmond Dantès in *The Count of Monte Cristo* is rich beyond imagination, yet he must find peace with those who stole his earlier, happy, life. Rose DeWitt Bukater in the film *Titanic* is about to marry a fabulously rich heir, yet she feels trapped and unhappy.

Exercise 24: Hidden Need

Look back over your final moral pillar in Exercise 15, since this should relate in some way to your character's hidden need. You may need to go back and forth with the moral and the hidden need to fine-tune the connection. Free-write ideas for what your protagonist lacks within himself or herself: some emotional completion that he can obtain before the end of the story. Then summarize this hidden need in a few words.

Protagonist's Previous Wound

What caused the protagonist's hidden need? For a character arc, your protagonist may have an unhealed source of continuing pain: a wound that occurred before the story began, or perhaps in the prologue. If present, this wound is undeserved. It can be from a single event or, more commonly, an extended situation, and it often occurs during childhood. For example, Mitch McDeere in *The Firm* was brought up in a trailer park with an abusive father, a weak mother, and a brother who went to prison. It is no wonder that he values wealth and social status. Edmond Dantès in *The Count of Monte Cristo* lost his freedom, his fiancée, his career, and his youth. It is no wonder his anger burns white-hot against those who stole these things. After her father's death, Rose and her mother in *Titanic* lived a charade of remaining in the upper class despite being penniless, because the father left them "nothing but a good name." It is no wonder that she is tired of always behaving precisely so that no one finds her and her mother out.

Exercise 25: Protagonist's Previous Wound

Take a few minutes to free-write about what your protagonist's wound might have been. How does it affect him, even now? When you're ready, summarize the wound in a few words.

Fear

Your protagonist has fought at great cost to overcome his circumstances from the wound, but he is afraid it may happen again. Mitch McDeere in *The Firm* graduates at the top of his class at Harvard law school, but is afraid of becoming dirt poor again. Edmond Dantès in *The Count of Monte Cristo* escapes the Chateau D'If and finds an immense fortune, but is afraid that his earlier wrenching loss will ultimately and forever go unpunished. Rose and her mother in *Titanic* have barely been able to hold on to their social status, and Rose is afraid this is her last chance—if she doesn't marry Cal, the charade will quickly and irrevocably collapse.

Exercise 26: Fear

What horrible situation is your protagonist afraid will be replayed in his life? Free-write about possible outcomes. Then in one sentence describe what, specifically, he is afraid will happen to him if he isn't always careful.

Protagonist's Outer Identity

Because of his fear, your protagonist has developed a protective identity that helps him to manage life. This identity is how your character sees himself, and he clings to it in order to define himself to others. Identity can be comprised of age, gender, belief system, job, family—whatever your character thinks is necessary to describe who he is.

A good way to specifically articulate the character's identity is to explore what the character would not do, or the types of feelings he would not admit to, if it meant he'd have to give up his identity.

For example, Mitch McDeere in *The Firm* is a successful young lawyer who will do whatever it takes to become established; just don't ask him to question whether his firm's actions are morally correct. Edmond Dantès in *The Count of Monte Cristo* is a wealthy aristocrat who controls lives behind the scenes; just don't ask him to reveal his true identity. Rose in *Titanic* is a beautiful young woman about to marry for money and status; just don't ask her to break out of her comfortable life.

Exercise 27: Protagonist's Outer Identity

Take some time to explore who your protagonist thinks he is. What does he need to keep doing to advance his life in the way it is going? What sorts of thoughts or actions would he never do?

Summarize your protagonist's identity and something he would never do.

Protagonist's Core

The trick of the character arc is to strip away the protagonist's identity so that he can become who he truly is: his core. His identity protects him from exposing this core. The protagonist doesn't know what he needs to be complete.

For example, Mitch McDeere in *The Firm* originally became a lawyer because he loved the law, and he needs to remember this. Edmond Dantès in *The Count of Monte Cristo* is originally a kind, generous, and optimistic young man, and needs to learn the power of forgiveness so that he can receive peace and a new love. Rose in *Titanic* feels suffocated, and needs to live as a free woman not bound by society's obligations.

Exercise 28: Protagonist's Core

What sort of life would best suit your protagonist? What choices would he need to make to get there from here? These are involved questions that take time to work through. Free-write your thoughts. Then, write down in a few words the essence or core of your character.

Author's Bargain

As a writer, you must be cruel to your protagonist. You are going to offer him the life of his dreams, but the catch is he must give up his identity in order to grab it. For example, Mitch in *The Firm* must give up a lucrative job manipulating the law if he is ever going to be able to truly practice law. Edmond Dantès in *The Count of Monte Cristo* must forgive if he wants peace. Rose in *Titanic* must break with Cal and her past if she is ever going to be with Jack.

Exercise 29: Author's Bargain

Think about the bargain you are going to strike with your protagonist. Give him everything he wants... but only if he gives up his old life. Summarize this bargain in a few words.

Other Characters

There are three character roles, or types, that are not essential, yet you should strongly consider including in your story.

Confidante

The confidante is someone with whom the protagonist confides, someone who shares the protagonist's journey to a greater or lesser extent. The confidante can be anyone—friend, coworker, spouse, lover, relative, employee, mentor, neighbor, whomever— who listens to the protagonist, gives him feedback, confronts or soothes him, and suggests solutions to problems. The protagonist gives this character regular updates and shares the deepest parts of his impressions and plans.

The confidante helps the protagonist achieve the story goal. Additionally, the confidante reveals the protagonist's inner struggle to him, and helps to point him in the direction of fulfilling his core.

Antagonist Character

In my opinion, all stories should personify their chief obstacle. Even if your protagonist's chief problem is a roaring fire, say, or a space mission gone bad, it is easiest to have a person (or sentient alien) for most of the story standing in the way. A great example of this is *Jaws*. Brody, the police chief, recognizes there is a big shark eating people. However his chief obstacle for three-quarters of the movie is the mayor who refuses to close the beaches. It is only in Act 3 that Brody actually goes to confront and destroy the fish. In *Titanic*, Rose deals with many obstacles, but it is only in Act 3 that she has to deal with a sinking boat.

According to John Truby, author of *The Anatomy of Story*, the antagonist pursues the same ultimate goal as the protagonist. For example, in *Jaws* both Brody and the mayor battle over who will control the town. In *Titanic* Rose battles with her mother and especially with Cal over who will control her life.

Romantic Interest

The romantic interest is a wonderful device to add tension to a story, and acts as the object of the protagonist's pursuit. On the inner level, the romantic interest is the protagonist's reward for overcoming his identity—the romantic interest will stay with him once his core is exposed.

In fact, often a romance develops when the romantic interest sees the protagonist's core underneath his identity, and this is why she sticks with him while he's ironing out his emotional wrinkles.

Exercise 30: Adding Other Characters

Take some time to free-write about how the confidante, antagonist character, and romantic interest types might fit with the story you're imagining. Do you already have one or more characters that might fit these roles? Can you add any? This may take a bit of time to work out, but adding one or more of these roles (preferably all three) will make planning and writing your story easier.

Summary

Exercise 31: Integrating your Four Story Pillars

Take some time to review your story pillars, and make sure they interlock and work together. Tweak them to fit. The stronger you can interconnect your story pillars, the more gripping your story will be. Although daunting, rewrite the exercises in the past three chapters if you need to. You will be grateful later that you prepared the ground for your story so well now.

You've done a lot of hard work on this level. Hopefully you now have a clear idea of the boundaries, and a solid foundation, for your story. Even now, you've done more work than many writers do before starting the actual writing, and your preparation will pay off soon. Congratulations! The next level goes into the essence of story structure as we study the universal shape of story.

LEVEL THREE:

Structure

You are now on the third level of story construction. On this level you're going to use the story template to form a strong frame for your story. This level may surprise you as you recognize things you never knew you knew about how a story flows.

Chapter Five

Explanation of the Story Template

In my studies of structure, the biggest surprise I found was how little story development varies. No matter the genre, the same shape of story kept appearing. By understanding this deep structure, you as a writer can eliminate the irrelevant and make sure that what you write is complete and proportional.

This three-act structure is not original with me: Aristotle first described it, and many write about it. I was skeptical, but during my studies I verified this. The explanation of the template in this book goes beyond anything I read, though, since I also made original observations in my studies. Blake Snyder's brilliant book *Save the Cat!* came closest to articulating what I was finding.

While you may find exceptions of component placement in the occasional story, these are few and minor compared to the overlying template structure. This template is virtually always present in the modern narrative—if you show me a story, I'll show you this progression.

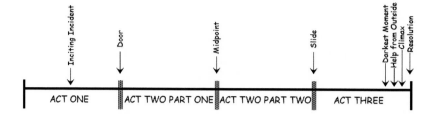

The story can be divided into four more-or-less equal parts, each with one or more distinct themes. Furthermore, the story posts occur reliably in the progression of the story.

I will use three well-known but different genre films to illustrate the template: *My Big Fat Greek Wedding*, *Star Wars*, and *The Wizard of Oz*.

Act One

Act one demonstrates the original or starting position of the protagonist, plus the set up to show how he moves into the main story. It's divided into three sub-parts:

Ordinary World

This portion occurs during the first ten to fifteen percent of the story, and shows what the protagonist's normal life is like. This life can represent a slow death of the character's dreams—he feels like he will never be able to escape to live the life he wants.

My Big Fat Greek Wedding: Toula is a thirty-year-old unmarried Greek woman working in her family's restaurant.

Star Wars: Luke is a frustrated young man who wants to attend the Academy, but must instead help his aunt and uncle farm on a backwater desert planet, Tatooine.

Wizard of Oz: Dorothy lives with her Uncle Henry and Auntie Em, and her dog Toto, in the middle of nowhere (Kansas).

Story Post: Inciting Incident

This occurs about ten to fifteen percent of the way through the story. The inciting incident shows a potential change offered to the protagonist, either a choice or an assignment. Usually the inciting incident is for a bridging goal, i.e. an intermediate goal that leads to the story goal.

My Big Fat Greek Wedding: Toula finds a college brochure that might offer her an opportunity to achieve something different by taking a few classes.

Star Wars: Luke finds Obi Wan Kenobi to interpret a secret message he found on an R2D2 droid that projects the image of a young woman. Obi Wan proposes that he and Luke help her.

Wizard of Oz: Because Dorothy's dog Toto bit Miss Gulch, she takes him to be destroyed.

Argument

This is the second part of the first act. In the argument phase, the protagonist must decide, or must make preparations, or must overcome obstacles, before he accepts the challenge of the inciting incident.

My Big Fat Greek Wedding: Toula must convince her father to allow her to take courses at the college. Toula's mother promises to help Toula, then manipulates her father to say "yes."

Star Wars: Luke finds that Storm Troopers have killed his aunt and uncle and are searching for the droids. He decides to escape with Obi Wan, but they need to find a transport ship. They go to Mos Eisley spaceport filled with strange aliens and meet with pilot Han Solo and the wookie Chewbacca.

Wizard of Oz: Toto escapes from Miss Gulch and runs back to Dorothy. Dorothy runs away, but a kindly traveler convinces her to go back home. She needs to hurry before a tornado hits.

Story Post: The Door

The door is located about one quarter of the way through the story. This is the last part of Act One, and shows a journey that the protagonist takes to enter the new world. The character of the door varies—it can be one line, or an elaborate three-scene set-up for something like, say, a rocket launch.

My Big Fat Greek Wedding: There are montage shots of the college campus of which Toula is now a member.

Star Wars: Luke and Obi Wan blast off with Han Solo, Chewbacca, and the droids C3PO and R2D2, just ahead of the storm troopers. They are going to the planet Alderaan to rescue Princess Leia.

Wizard of Oz: Dorothy makes it to her house just before the tornado lifts it up. The house lands in the new world of Oz, and Dorothy disembarks.

Act Two/Part One

During this second quarter of the story, the protagonist learns how the new world works, often shown as a series of three or four increasingly involved encounters. During this section the protagonist has the sense (even if unspoken) that once this journey is over he will simply return to his old way of life with some memories, but essentially unchanged.

My Big Fat Greek Wedding: Toula is shown changing her image to become more glamorous (hair, clothing, contacts, makeup etc.), answering questions competently in class, and socializing with other students—something she couldn't do as a kid.

Star Wars: Luke is instructed by Obi Wan in the Force, Han teaches points of space travel, and the droids adapt to the ship and learn chess strategies for Wookies. Obi Wan senses something terrible has happened.

Wizard of Oz: Dorothy meets Glinda the good witch of the North, puts on the ruby slippers, and starts off down the yellow brick road. Along the way she meets the scarecrow who wants a brain, the tin man who wants a heart, and the lion who wants courage.

Story Post: The Midpoint

This is the last sequence of act two/part one, occurring between fifty and sixty percent of the way through the story. It is often an exciting, flashy event. The midpoint is either a false high or a devastating loss that makes it clear that the protagonist can no longer go back to his Ordinary World unchanged.

My Big Fat Greek Wedding: Toula meets Ian, a high school English teacher. Although she knows her family will never accept him because he isn't Greek, she starts dating him. Toula's cousin Nikki tells Toula that the family knows about her romance with Ian, and she must break it off.

Star Wars: The *Millennium Falcon* comes out of light speed into an asteroid field—the planet Alderaan has been destroyed by the Death Star, an enormous circulating enemy ship. They are pulled inside by tractor beam.

Wizard of Oz: When Dorothy and her new friends approach Oz, the Wicked Witch of the West conjures a field of poppies that cause Dorothy and the lion to fall asleep. Glinda causes snow that counteracts the poppies' effects.

Act Two/Part Two

This is usually the most difficult part of the story to write since it tends to be comprised of many small narratives that are densely interwoven. Much variability occurs in the presentation of this section. However three general themes often appear:

Hidden Need Triplet

Although the three components of the hidden need triplet may be interspersed throughout act two/part two and act three, they more often appear as a block right after the midpoint. The block forms a small contained story that strategically gives the audience a break from the story tension engendered by the exciting, and exhausting, midpoint. The triplet solves the protagonist's hidden need (see Exercise 24) in a three-part sequence: the hidden need is shown, the hidden need is solved, and the hidden need is demonstrated to be solved.

My Big Fat Greek Wedding: Toula's hidden need, that she must accept her family, isn't solved until act three when her grandmother gives her an heirloom bridal crown to wear for her wedding. This demonstrates a variant of the hidden need solution appearing near or at the Climax.

Star Wars: Luke's hidden need is that he must trust himself to lead.

Demonstration of Hidden Need: Luke, Han, and Chewbacca rescue Leia from the prison cell, and because there is no escape plan Leia must take control. She blasts a hole into a garbage chute.

Hidden Need is Solved: Luke is pulled into the muck by a serpent that lives there; after struggling he resurfaces. Then the garbage chute starts compressing and Luke takes control to call C3P0 to shut down the compactors.

Hidden Need is Demonstrated to be Solved: They escape, then Luke and Leia separate from Han and Chewbacca. Luke stops an attack by locking the controls on a door, then grabs Leia to swing across a chasm.

Wizard of Oz: Dorothy's hidden need is to appreciate being home.

Demonstration of Hidden Need: Not explicitly shown in act two/part two, but clearly demonstrated beforehand with Dorothy's statements and running away from home.

Hidden Need is Solved: Dorothy enters the Emerald City. When she is told she can't see the wizard to get home, she cries and says she didn't appreciate Auntie Em when she was with her.

Hidden Need is Demonstrated to be Solved: Dorothy is kidnapped by the witch, then sees Auntie Em in the witch's crystal ball. Dorothy calls to Auntie Em to say she's frightened and wants to be with her.

Antagonists Get Stronger

This theme was pointed out by Blake Snyder in his book *Save the Cat!* Following the midpoint, the antagonists are in ascendancy. Their strength is maximally demonstrated here.

My Big Fat Greek Wedding: Toula's family tries to break up her relationship with Ian and to match her with suitable Greek bachelors.

Star Wars: The Death Star is now functional, and the leaders make plans to destroy a rebel outpost. Meanwhile, storm troopers on the Death Star systematically discover different members of Luke's little band and chase them. Darth Vader knows that Obi Wan is present on the Death Star and goes to look for him.

Wizard of Oz: The witch orders her flying monkeys to kidnap Dorothy and Toto. Once in the castle, the witch sets an hourglass to mark Dorothy's remaining time to live.

Protagonist Disintegrates

After the midpoint, the protagonist has trouble finding his equilibrium.

My Big Fat Greek Wedding: Ian proposes to Toula and yields to the powerful family forces by joining the Greek Orthodox Church and being baptized. Ian and his conservative parents attend a celebratory lamb roast and party enjoyed by Toula's multiple, rowdy, relatives.

Star Wars: Luke's small band isn't sure how they're going to survive the next few minutes, much less escape.

Wizard of Oz: Dorothy is intimidated by the wizard of Oz, and then captured by the witch.

Story Post: Slide

This is the last sequence of act two/part two, and occurs at about the three-quarter mark. Often another flashy event, it spins the story into a new direction and funnels the options so that the nature of the climax is clearly seen. Furthermore, Snyder identifies the "whiff of death" here where a symbolic or real death is shown.

My Big Fat Greek Wedding: Toula comes home with her wedding plans, only to learn her family has already ordered the invitations and the bridesmaids' dresses. Toula now sees that, although she's tried valiantly, she will never be free of her family—her sense of independence has been killed. The nature of the climax is centered on the actual wedding.

Star Wars: While Luke and company make their way back to the *Millennium Falcon*, Obi Wan steps out to duel with Darth Vader and sacrifices himself. Darth Vader cuts him down. The nature of the climax is centered on destroying the Death Star from which Luke's group is escaping.

Wizard of Oz: Dorothy and company confront the Wicked Witch of the West in her castle, and Dorothy melts her by dousing her with water. Dorothy and friends take the witch's broom to present to the Wizard of Oz. The nature of the climax is centered on the Wizard of Oz.

Act Three

The protagonist gets ready for the final encounter with the antagonist, although it seems unlikely that he will ever win. There are further setbacks for the protagonist, and further victories for the antagonist. If a member of the protagonist's party has disappeared or been captured, she may reappear toward the beginning of this act to join in with this last series of conflicts. This act has two parts: preparation for battle, then an ending series of conflicts with secondary antagonists and finally the primary antagonist.

Crazy Plan

The protagonist typically develops a crazy plan to vanquish the antagonist—the protagonist identifies an unlikely weakness, and wonders how he might be able to exploit this.

My Big Fat Greek Wedding: Toula resigns herself to dealing with her family (no crazy plan).

Star Wars: The rebels identify a miniscule vulnerability in the Death Star: a shielded channel three feet wide that nevertheless will set off a complete explosion if a bomb can be dropped directly inside.

Wizard of Oz: Dorothy will set sail in a balloon with the wizard back to Kansas.

Ending Series of Battles

The final battle sequence is usually prolonged, with three or more stages of the battle between protagonist and antagonist. During the battles the protagonist might make some headway, but this is offset by catastrophic losses. The antagonist is stronger and seems most likely to win. Toward the end of the climax events funnel into a stereotyped sequence of the following story posts:

Story Post: Darkest Moment

The darkest moment describes the worst position the protagonist can possibly imagine. All of his fears about the antagonist are about to come true. There may be even worse consequences than the protagonist has heretofore dreamed possible: not only will he die, but others will be hurt.

My Big Fat Greek Wedding: On the morning of the wedding Toula prepares with her entire family and realizes she will never be free.

Star Wars: Luke in his X-wing fighter sees that the Death Star is in range of the Rebel Base and ready to destroy it. Most of his fellow flyers have been shot down. He is trying to fly into the channel, but is almost out of control as enemy ships shoot at him.

Wizard of Oz: The Wizard promises to take Dorothy in his balloon to Kansas, but he accidently releases the balloon and flies away without her.

Story Post: Help from Outside

This story post was identified for me at a writer's conference from a NANGIE course taught by authors Nancy Rue and Angela Hunt. Help from outside is a small action from someone or something outside the protagonist that allows him to regroup and win. This help does not cause the protagonist to win, but offers an opportunity.

My favorite help from outside is in the movie *Facing the Giants*. A small high school football team amazingly finds itself in the state playoffs against a monster team, and in the last few seconds to win must make a fifty-some yard field goal. The field kicker is second string and has never approached this distance. He is even kicking into the wind. Then, there is a camera shot of the flag, showing that the wind has suddenly changed direction.

My Big Fat Greek Wedding: Toula's grandmother shows Toula her own wedding crown, and Toula realizes that her family all love her, and that she is connected to them in a deep and profound way. (This scene also solves Toula's hidden need).

Star Wars: As Luke struggles against the enemy ship, Han Solo suddenly appears in the *Millenium Falcon* to clear the area. Then Luke has one last shot to drop the bomb that will destroy the Death Star. As he engages his computer targeting sequence, he hears Obi Wan's voice saying, "Trust your feelings."

Wizard of Oz: Glinda appears and tells Dorothy she already has the answer to get home.

Story Post: Climax

This can be quick or prolonged and is often flashy. By gaining strength from the help from outside, the protagonist engages one final time with the antagonist and ultimately wins: if not the outer conflict, then certainly the inner (think *Rocky*).

My Big Fat Greek Wedding: Toula and Ian have a beautiful, Greek, wedding and reception. Toula's father makes a joke that shows how Toula's family and Ian's family, although different, are ultimately the same.

Star Wars: Luke evades Darth Vader to drop the bomb into the channel, thereby blowing up the Death Star.

Wizard of Oz: Dorothy clicks her heels three times to return to Kansas.

Story Post: Resolution

This final scene or two shows how the protagonist's life will go on now that he has solved the story problem.

My Big Fat Greek Wedding: Toula and Ian are shown several years later in a house next to her parents' house, walking their daughter to Greek school. Toula tells her daughter she has to learn Greek as part of her heritage, but she can marry anyone she wants to.

Star Wars: Luke, Han, and Chewbacca receive medals from Princess Leia in a grand ceremony.

Wizard of Oz: After apparently hitting her head during the tornado, Dorothy wakes in her bed in Kansas, and is happy and content to be back home with Uncle Henry, Auntie Em, and Toto. The traveling salesman and the three farmhands stop by to make sure she's fine.

Chapter Six

Writing with the Story Template

Now that you've seen this template structure, you need to verify it and be able to work comfortably with it. In this chapter you'll assemble the template for your own story.

Exercise 32: Studying the Template

Select three or more movies and/or novels with which you're familiar. Going through them again, and using a watch or page numbers to assist if you want, identify, describe, and write down the following story posts and story points for each:

Ordinary World, Inciting Incident, Bridging Story Goal, Argument, Door, Story Goal, New World, Midpoint, Hidden Need, Slide, Crazy Plan, Darkest Moment, Help from Outside, Climax, Resolution.

Hopefully you now believe the template works. In the next section you will organize your own template story.

Act One

The body of act one includes three parts: ordinary world, inciting incident, and argument. This act ends with the story post of the door, a journey of some sort that takes the protagonist into the new world.

Exercise 33: Ordinary World

Describe your protagonist's ordinary world. Does his ordinary world represent a slow death, and if so, how? Is he aware of this? Does he long for something he feels he will never achieve? What keeps him in these circumstances? Who else is part of the ordinary world? Free-write your thoughts. Summarize the ordinary world in a sentence, and write some ideas for demonstrating this world to your audience.

Exercise 34: Inciting Incident

Write a few ideas for your story's inciting incident: the event that is presented to the protagonist as an opportunity for him to stretch beyond his ordinary world. Who or what presents it? This is often a seemingly small or even inconsequential opportunity that you the author know will lead to a big change. What is the bridging story goal that the inciting incident establishes? Free-write your thoughts, and then summarize the inciting incident in a sentence.

Exercise 35: Argument

The argument represents the delay the protagonist must experience before accepting the invitation of the inciting incident. He may be reluctant to take the invitation, experience obstacles to accepting it, and/or need time to prepare. Please note that the protagonist isn't pushed into the new world, but must actively accept the opportunity offered to him here. Psychologically if the protagonist wouldn't accept this opportunity, then you the author must continue to narrow his options until this is his only choice.

Free-write your thoughts, and then summarize the internal and external obstacles that prevent your protagonist from immediately accepting the invitation.

Exercise 36: Door

The door is the final section of act one, and represents a journey into the new world of act two. This journey may be only a few lines, or can be an elaborate sequence of events. What does your protagonist's journey look like? Free-write your thoughts, and then summarize them in a sentence.

Act Two/Part One

The theme of act two/part one is for the protagonist to learn about the new world he has just entered. This quarter usually has three or four, increasingly complex, encounters with aspects of the new world and/or antagonist. This quarter ends with the story post of the midpoint, either a false high or a disaster.

Your protagonist usually meets friends and allies in this quarter who will remain with him during his journey.

In the new world, theme changes between the old world and the new are explored: for example going from present to past, alone to together, material to spiritual values, fear to faith, and so forth.

Exercise 37: New Encounters

The protagonist's encounters demonstrate different aspects of the new world, such as new friends made, powers opposed, and general adjustments to a different environment. These encounters escalate, and the last moves directly into the midpoint. Free-write about theme changes in the new world and some adjustments your protagonist might make as he explores this new environment. At the end, summarize possible encounters in one sentence each.

Midpoint

The midpoint occurs between fifty and sixty percent of the way through the story, and represents a turning point. Before the midpoint, the protagonist has the sense (even if unspoken) that after the new world he would or could return unchanged to his ordinary world. The midpoint changes things so that the protagonist's course is permanently altered, whether through a wedding, a bomb exploding, or a realization about a previously unsuspected person.

There are two types of midpoints. The type of midpoint—false high or disaster—should be chosen based on when the protagonist realizes he will eventually confront the antagonist. The first type—the disaster midpoint—is typically used if some aspects of the ultimate enemy or the final climax are known to the protagonist before the midpoint. For example, in the film *U571* the American officers know from the beginning that they are fighting the Nazis, so the final climax must have something to do with them. The disaster midpoint occurs when the American submarine is blown up and the captain is drowned, leaving Ryan in command. Disaster midpoints are most common, and there are many examples.

On the other hand, the second type—the false high midpoint—is used if the ultimate enemy or type of climax isn't revealed to the protagonist until after the midpoint. In other words, the protagonist will be surprised after the midpoint to learn that he will, indeed, need to fight a final battle. The story taking place before the midpoint involves the protagonist's adaptation to an exotic set of circumstances or theme changes of the new world. For example, in the film *Sky High* Will must learn how to be a superhero although he hasn't yet exhibited special powers. The false high midpoint occurs when Will in front of cheering spectators is able to "save the citizen" using newly-discovered super strength. Only after this midpoint does the antagonist who wants to destroy Will's parents begin to interact with him. Another good example of a false high midpoint is Stephen King's *The Dead Zone*, when Johnny Smith holds a surprising news conference right before his mother dies. This false high type of midpoint is not as common as the disaster type midpoint.

Exercise 38: Midpoint

The identification of the primary antagonist and/or the general nature of the climax is an important marker—will it be clear to the protagonist from the beginning that a fight is brewing with a particular enemy or force (disaster midpoint), or is the protagonist surprised after the middle of the story that he will need to fight a final confrontation of some sort (false high midpoint)? Free-write your ideas for the midpoint, and how the midpoint might change the course of your story. Summarize your thoughts in one sentence.

Act Two/Part Two

This is usually the most difficult quarter of the story to write. Although this section exhibits much structural variability between stories, there are a few tricks you can use to fill this quarter while maintaining tension. Act two/part two often has three separate themes: hidden need triplet, antagonists get stronger, and protagonist disintegrates after midpoint. There is also usually a "How Bad is the Antagonist" beat.

The last section of this quarter is the slide, another turning point in which the story spins into a new direction. The slide clearly shows the nature of the final climax, and also contains Snyder's "whiff of death."

Exercise 39: Hidden Need Triplet

This triplet forms a little switched-away story after the high midpoint tension: an effective psychological device. The triplet's three parts are hidden need is demonstrated, hidden need is solved, and hidden need is shown to be solved.

Free-write about your protagonist's hidden need. Determine what sorts of scenes might clearly demonstrate it, other scenes of how your protagonist will have his attention drawn to his hidden need, and finally scenes that show him confronting a small problem using his new way of thinking. Once you have your ideas, list them, then summarize your best ones into a single sentence each.

Exercise 40: Antagonists Get Stronger and "How Bad is the Antagonist" Beat

Your primary and secondary antagonists are successful as they form plans and prepare for battle. The obstacles to the story goal for the protagonist are shown to be formidable.

Often a single scene in this section will epitomize the worst, most fearful destruction of which the primary antagonist is capable. This is called the "How Bad is the Antagonist" beat. The circumstances can be experienced by a mirror character (someone who is similar to the protagonist), may be described or shown in a vision, or otherwise made real to your audience if not necessarily to your protagonist.

Free-write some obstacles that your antagonists may generate, as well as other external obstacles from the story world or plot. What plans are your antagonists forming? What might be the scariest, most evil thing the primary antagonist can think of doing to someone? At the end, make a list of these external obstacles.

Exercise 41: Protagonist Disintegrates

The protagonist has just experienced a major upheaval from the midpoint, and needs to find a new balance. He feels as if he is scrambling to stay ahead, and his chances are dim. He may find clues to the antagonist's weaknesses but doesn't see how these clues can help him. You the author will use these clues to help the protagonist form a crazy plan in act three.

Free-write some internal and external obstacles that your protagonist will face in this section. Some of these obstacles, especially the external, may overlap from the previous section. Then, summarize these in a list.

Exercise 42: Slide

The slide is the last section of act two/part two, and spins the story into a new direction. Possibilities for the story ending funnel at this point into a single, final battle that looms on the horizon—if not before, it will be clear to your audience now that the story goal will be unequivocally answered, yes or no, through this final conflict between the protagonist and antagonist. There is also Snyder's "whiff of death" here, in which a symbolic or real death occurs.

Free-write some ideas for what your slide will look like, then summarize the slide in a sentence.

Act Three

Following the slide, events continue to go poorly for your protagonist although he keeps fighting and has a few small victories. Your protagonist develops a crazy plan using his own ingenuity and any clues to antagonist weakness he found in act two/part two. He holds a dim hope that he might, just might, be able to win. Still, circumstances are grim and growing worse. Finally the protagonist is about to die, but through a small help from outside is able to muster forces for one last battle, and succeeds in some way or fashion. This final sequence is comparable to the big fireworks crescendo at the end of the display.

Exercise 43: Crazy Plan

The protagonist realizes that he is outmatched by the antagonist and will not be able to win using conventional tactics. He comes up with a plan that seems unlikely, but if every circumstance lines up exactly right he might, just might, be able to defeat the antagonist. This plan is his only hope.

Free-write about how your protagonist may be able to defeat your antagonist, and what the crazy plan might look like. Then, summarize your ideas into a sentence or two.

Exercise 44: Preparation for Battle

After the slide, the beginning of this last quarter shows the protagonist getting into a progressively worse position while the antagonist succeeds in getting more aspects of his plan into place. There may be a few bright spots—for example, if a member of the protagonist's team has disappeared, he or she may reappear here. The general mood is grim determination while preparing to fight an impossible battle using the crazy plan. There is usually no direct contact between protagonist and antagonist yet. Free-write about several sequential problems and/or preparations that can appear, and then summarize these in a list.

Exercise 45: Battle

Finally, it's time for the protagonist and antagonist to directly engage. While they may or may not have had a few minor tangles before, this is the major interaction. This final sequence is most effective if you have three or even more varied conflicts back to back.

Free-write about what your final sequence might look like. Then, summarize the events in a list.

Exercise 46: Darkest Moment

The progression of events in the battle moves to where your protagonist is about to lose everything he ever wanted in the story, and then some. He is only waiting for the antagonist to finish him off.

Free-write about this darkest moment, and then summarize, very specifically, what it is.

Exercise 47: Help from Outside

Right when the protagonist is about to die, literally or figuratively, a small help from outside inspires him to fight once more. This help can be a memory, a movement from the crowd that distracts the antagonist for a second, a tool suddenly appearing, or anything else that momentarily shifts the balance. This help does not cause the protagonist to win, but gives him a chance or strength or inspiration that allows him to go ahead just one more time.

Free-write about possible helps from outside. At the end, summarize your thoughts in a single sentence.

Exercise 48: Climax

This is the final, pitched battle between protagonist and antagonist. There may be back and forth, but ultimately the protagonist gains the edge and finally defeats the antagonist or otherwise wins. There may be the culmination of a "gift at climax" subplot to help the protagonist win (discussed in Chapter Eight). The climax can be bittersweet, but the protagonist gains the story goal or a comparable victory within it. Sometimes in a moral decision the protagonist gives up the original story goal.

Free-write some possible exchanges in this final, pitched battle. At the end, list your thoughts succinctly and clearly. State what the protagonist has lost, and what he has won.

Exercise 49: Resolution

Finally, you need to show how your protagonist's life will go on now that he has solved his hidden need and the final encounter is over. Some stories have a fillip, a final event or piece of information that ties an unexpected end or casts the story events into a new light. A common fillip is the clichéd hint that the antagonist may rise again to threaten the protagonist or others.

Free-write to explore how your story will end, and if you might be able to include a fillip or other ironic circumstance. Finally, summarize your thoughts in a sentence or two.

Conclusion

This template forms a strong framework for your story, and ensures that you've included all the critical points.

Chapter Seven

Character Template

The Character Arc also has a template or pattern that it follows throughout a story. I found that the stages of this pattern usually are not completely demonstrated in the story. However, determining this pattern, whether you show it or not, is a helpful tool for you the author to learn about your protagonist and to walk through his story with him. In this chapter you'll review this development and figure out how your own characters will change and grow.

Character Arc

I discussed the character arc in detail in Chapter Four; here's a quick review. In the character arc, the character may have a wound from before the story begins (sometimes shown in the prologue) that he has compensated for with great difficulty. His adaptive response gives him an identity, a role, which defines him. For example, in the film *Shrek*, Shrek lives with everything an ogre could want in his swamp. In the film *Titanic* Rose is a high-society young lady about to marry a wealthy heir. However, the character's adaptive response to the wound, while allowing him to function in the world, doesn't solve his deep emotional need of which he isn't aware. For example, Shrek longs for companionship and possibly love. Rose longs to live free, not in the restrictive world of class. Who the character really is, deep inside, is called the core.

The character arc follows the gradual stripping away of the protagonist's outer identity so that his longing or need can be integrated into a better form of life. If you have a romantic interest for the protagonist, this interest character usually falls in love with your protagonist because she can see his core beyond the outer identity.

I adapted much of this character arc from Michael Hauge's articulate explanation in *The Hero's 2 Journeys*.

In the story there are generally six stages to a character arc.

Stage One: Set-Up

This stage occurs during the ordinary world section of the template, in which your protagonist exists completely in his identity. Your character's romantic interest (if present) is attracted to your character because she sees his inner core beyond the tough exterior.

For example, Shrek lives alone in the middle of his swamp. Rose is shown wearing a big hat that covers her face as she dismounts from the car arrived at the port with the *Titanic*.

Exercise 50: Character Identity

Free-write to describe your character's identity. Imagine some small set-ups or scenes that might show, not tell, the character's outer persona.

Stage Two: A Glimpse of the Longing

This stage takes place during the argument phase of act one. The protagonist has a glimpse of what it might be like to live within his core.

For example, Shrek chases off the woodland creatures from his swamp, but instead of running away they briefly applaud him as if he were a friend. He shrugs it off. Rose is taken with Jack's passionate sketches.

Exercise 51: Glimpse

What is your protagonist's core? Imagine some ways to show, not tell, a quick glimpse that your protagonist may take.

Stage Three: Straddling

During the second quarter of the story (act two/part one) the protagonist moves toward his core without losing his identity. He enjoys playing at living a life according to his core, although he "knows" this could never be a permanent situation. The confidante character, if present, also reveals the protagonist's core to him.

For example, Shrek and Donkey are accompanying Princess Fiona back to Lord Farquaad. Donkey, the confidante, asks Shrek why he doesn't just tell Fiona he loves her, but Shrek says she would never love him back. Still, Shrek enjoys pretending that this time of being with Fiona will last. Rose enjoys dancing with Jack below decks with the third class passengers.

Exercise 52: Straddling

Free-write a few possible actions that would show your protagonist playing at living his core.

Stage Four: Fear

In the third quarter of the story (act two/part two), the protagonist is fully committed to living his core, but fear grows that he won't be able to do it. The protagonist jettisons his identity, but at the end of this stage retreats back.

For example, Shrek tells Donkey that yes, he could love Fiona, but then hears her talking terribly about ogres. Shrek doesn't realize that Fiona is talking about her own hideous enchantment, not about Shrek. Shrek happily delivers Fiona to Lord Farquaad and tells Donkey to leave him alone. Rose runs away with Jack, but when the *Titanic* is filling one of the last lifeboats, she gets on with the rich people.

Exercise 53: Fear

Free-write about how your protagonist might expose his core and throw away his identity in order to permanently live this way. Then imagine situations causing him to seemingly reject this new life to retreat back to his old identity.

Stage Five: Living One's Truth, With Everything to Lose

Finally the protagonist decides that, darn it, he's going to live his core instead of his identity. He will be who he really is, and find his destiny no matter what. For example, Shrek decides that he will rescue Fiona from her marriage to Lord Farquaad even though he doesn't know that Fiona loves him. Rose jumps out of the lifeboat to be with Jack on the *Titanic* even though it's going to sink in a few minutes. This moment occurs close to or at the story climax, achieving the story goal and realizing the character's core.

Exercise 54: Living the Core

Free-write some possible scenarios that demonstrate your protagonist's commitment to his core, no matter what.

Stage Six: Journey is Completed

This stage shows the results of the protagonist's actions: his new life will proceed in a different channel now that he has realized who he truly is. His destiny has been achieved.

For example, Shrek and Fiona, two ogres, marry and go back to the swamp to live. Jack dies, but Rose survives the *Titanic's* sinking and goes on to live a full life as Jack would have lived it with her.

Exercise 55: Destiny

Free-write what your protagonist's life will look like by living his core instead of his identity. How is he fulfilled?

A Final Note

I want to make a quick observation here in regards to the character arc. I used the film *The Titanic* because this clearly demonstrates my point.

It is this: the character arc describes the protagonist's fulfillment, and the author can push this into a selfish focus if he isn't careful. For example, I would argue that Rose in the course of pursuing her dream behaves immorally throughout the story arc, and ends up hurting many people, not the least of whom is Jack.

The story is a powerful medium because it bypasses logical defenses to penetrate to the emotions. As the author, you have a responsibility to employ moral and edifying themes that will strengthen your audience. This, I believe, is the purpose of art.

I would encourage you as the writer to choose moral actions and moral goals for your characters to pursue. Sacrifice is a potent quality in story, as in life, and sometimes the most powerful turn for a story is when the character denies himself in order to benefit others. Think about that.

LEVEL FOUR:

Adding Complexity

You are now on the fourth level of story construction. On this level you're going to formulate subplots that reinforce themes, complicate the plot, deepen characters, and overall enrich your story. This level also includes a comprehensive story review that will allow you to generate most or all of your raw material. When you've finished this level, you'll have some amazing ideas. Don't worry about the chaos—in the next level you'll integrate this material into a unified narrative for your story.

Chapter Eight

Characters and Subplots

Recurring Characters

In a full-length story there are generally about eight to ten clearly identifiable, recurring characters. Although some of these are main characters, others are simply unique recurring characters providing a backdrop for the story.

For example, *Star Wars* has Luke, Obi-Wan, Han Solo, Chewbacca, Princess Leia, R2D2, C3PO, and Darth Vader. In two later films the Emperor is added. Additional characters that wouldn't count as being recurring include Luke's aunt and uncle, the director of the Death Star, and the Rebel commanders and other Rebel fighters.

In *Rocky*, the characters are Rocky, Adrienne, Paulie, Mickey, Apollo Creed, the manager who works with Apollo to organize the fights, Rocky's loan shark boss, and the little girl whom Rocky walks home (more or less, but she has a memorable role). In *My Big Fat Greek Wedding*, the characters are Toula, Ian, Ian's parents,

Toula's mother and father, Ian's schoolteacher friend, Nikki, Toula's aunt, Toula's brother, and Toula's grandmother. I might argue that Ian's parents count as one character since they are indistinguishable story-wise, although this point isn't important.

In stories there are, to be sure, other characters besides these recurring ones, but they move in the background to give a sense of the story world without a definite sense of uniqueness. They don't alter the plot. The judgment call of who, exactly, is an identifiable character in an established story may be subjective, but doesn't matter except in your own opinion as you construct your story. This device of character identification simply gives you a guideline to develop characters in a balanced fashion, and delivers a rough feel of how much "stuff" you want to include.

Exercise 56: Story Characters

Who are your story characters? Free-write a list of all of the people who might be in your story, whether they are major actors or simply recurring bit players. How many do you have? The eight to ten figure is a good rule of thumb for unique, identifiable characters—it makes your story seem large enough without confusing the reader or viewer. Note that this figure doesn't include walk-on characters such as the waitress or the taxi driver.

Now, go over your list to refine it. If you need to, redo your list. Label the general author purpose for including each character. Some examples are protagonist, romantic interest, confidante, antagonist, secondary antagonist, comic relief, etc.

Subplots

Subplots are miniature related stories that occur between or within the actions of your main story. They are used to increase plot tension, explore character, and/or deepen theme. Since they are often stories or story-like, they can follow an abbreviated story structure.

The driving force of a story is its story goal.

Character Goals

What does each character want to achieve in the story? The protagonist's main goal is the story goal. He also should have a second goal that relates in some way to his hidden need. For example, he wants to win the romantic interest's love, or he wants to become an effective leader, or he wants to redeem his family's name.

Your other characters also have lives of their own. For example, the protagonist's love interest may want to get a break in her singing career before she's pulled into the main story. Even in a team- or military-type story, with everyone focused on the story goal, each character should have some personality and dream they want to achieve after the story is over. You don't have to include these minor character goals in your final story, but you the author should know them.

Exercise 57: Character Goals

Referring to your character list from Exercise 56, write down what each character wants in your story. Make each character goal concrete and unique to the individual. Don't have your characters focus on just reacting to the protagonist. You do not need to do this further development for your smallest recurring characters. Just pick the top four or five or so.

Story Strands

I found when doing my analyses of stories that the number of subplots varied depending on length, genre, and often the whim of the writer. However, even though multiple subplots appeared, so did order: plot or subplots fell into one of five general categories based on the purpose of the storyline. I call these five general categories the story strands:

A Strand: Main Plot
B Strand: Protagonist's Hidden Need
C Strand: Antagonist's Story
D Strand: Gift at Climax
E Strand: Protagonist's Mirror

More than one story strand can be followed in one scene. For example, a scene may develop a subplot character at the same time that it pushes ahead the main story line.

Each of these strands (except A) can hold up to about three story lines or subplots. I advise caution against loading your story too heavily with subplots, though—too many confuse the plot and diffuse the message. On the other hand, one or a few well-placed subplots beyond the hidden need can dramatically deepen your story. If you use them, the trick is to focus on coordinating them with other story elements. Subplots tend to be used more in longer works and/or more literary-type works. Even if you don't develop intricate subplots, you'll probably want to have, at the minimum, one abbreviated form for each of these strands except A. Let's take these strands one at a time.

A Strand: Main or External Story

The A strand is your plot pillar, complete with the story question and the template design as discussed in the previous level. You already know about this one.

B Strand: Hidden Need

Many stories have a protagonist with just one hidden need, but fairly frequently the protagonist has two hidden needs that are usually two parts of a whole. With two hidden needs, one tends to be an outer manifestation of the second, inner problem. One of them is typically solved right after the midpoint, and the second is solved at the exciting climactic point. Even if you only have a single hidden need in your story, a two-pronged approach to solution often appears: the hidden need is solved during act two/part two, and then the protagonist takes a critical action close to the climax stemming from this solution.

An example of the double hidden need is the film *Iron Will*. Will Stoneman is a teenage boy whose father has just died while training for an ambitious 500 mile dogsled race. Will decides to stand in for his father to win the money needed to save the homestead for his mother. He must learn to rely on himself rather than others, a hidden need that is solved on schedule right after the midpoint when he defends himself against the antagonist so that the antagonist will now leave him alone. However, Will also has a second hidden need: after his father broke through thin ice and drowned, Will became deathly afraid of taking his dog sled over rivers, sometimes handicapping himself in the race by trekking miles around the beaten trail. At the climactic sequence Will decisively bests the antagonist, but must also cross a frozen waterway to win the race. His hidden needs are related because solving them both allows Will to get past his father's death in order to rely on himself rather than others. The outer demonstration of crossing water is a symbolic journey demonstrating he is now whole.

Exercise 58: Hidden Need(s)

Looking at your previous exercises, review your protagonist's hidden need triplet (Exercise 39), help from outside (Exercise 47), and climax (Exercise 48). How might the solved hidden need from act two/part two become critical while confronting the climactic problem in act three? Should you add a second, related, hidden need? Free-write about possibilities.

Finally, summarize your hidden need(s) in a sentence or two.

C Strand: Antagonist Story

Much of a story can be thought of as a point-counterpoint exchange between the protagonist and obstacles. You therefore need to be clear not just on your protagonist's actions, but on those factors that block him from reaching his story goal.

This C strand covers all the counterpoints moving against the protagonist, whether antagonist, secondary antagonists, or forces coming together (a storm brewing, a decision being made by the board). Since the primary antagonist and other antagonists often have complex plans, you'll need to understand these plans to make them as strong as possible at as many points as possible, and then figure out surprising ways for the protagonist to escape.

At this level you need to start (or continue) thinking about the C strand, but you don't have to develop it in final detail until later.

Exercise 59: Obstacles

Review your story, then list as many internal and external obstacles for your protagonist as you can. Review your primary antagonist: psychologically, why is he doing what he is doing, and why does he think he's right? What surprising moves might he make against your protagonist? Review your other characters: which of these might form an obstacle to your protagonist at different parts of your story? Which ones are working with the primary antagonist? What do your characters want, and why do these wants oppose the protagonist's goal?

Free-write about the oppositions that your protagonist might experience, and discover how he might react to them. List ideas for point-counterpoint moves in your story. Describe what and why the bad guys are doing what they do.

D Strand: Gift at Climax

This is the first of two kinds of story strand that do not directly relate to the protagonist. The D strand is an external story that doesn't need to follow the steps of a typical story development (explained below), although it can. This strand delivers information, an important tool, or other form of help usually around the climax. The purpose of the D strand is to set up this help so that it is believable.

For example, in the film *The Two Towers*, Aragorn, Legolas, and Gimli are traveling to the Keep of Rohan because they know a big battle will be fought there. The wizard Gandalf tells them he will "return on the fifth day at sunrise," then rides off. During the battle the Keep is bravely defended but still about to fall (darkest moment). Aragorn and company decide to ride out to make one last, suicidal, stand at daybreak. As they ride out, Gandalf appears on a hill with another army, and the enemy is defeated.

Exercise 60: Gift at Climax

Review your notes of the climax (Exercise 48). How is your protagonist going to finally win? Will he need information or tools that won't easily be available? Remember that your protagonist has a crazy plan he implements in act three— is this plan sufficient to win against the antagonist, or will there be a final boost from a different (surprising) quarter that will allow him to win?

Free-write about possibilities for your D strand. At the end, summarize your thoughts in a sentence or two.

E Strand: Protagonist's Mirror

This is the second of two kinds of story strand that does not directly follow the protagonist. The stories in this strand are typically the ones thought of as being "subplots" in the general vernacular. The E strand is made of one or more internal stories of a mirror in which another character faces the same essential problem or choice as the protagonist. The most effective mirror technique has the subplot character solve the problem in a different, usually worse, way so that the reader can understand the stakes or consequences if the protagonist is not successful in his story goal. For example, in *Lord of the Ring*, Gollum is a hobbit ruined by wearing the One Ring for centuries, and is Frodo's mirror as Frodo is drawn to the Ring's power. Isildur was an ancient ruler of Gondor seduced by the Ring and unable to destroy it. He is Aragorn's mirror, since his failure makes Aragorn afraid that he cannot righteously wield power.

Your antagonist is also often a mirror character, although his story is covered in the C strand not E strand.

Truby's Seven Minimal Story Steps

John Truby, in his book *The Anatomy of Story*, describes the seven minimal steps of a story:

1. Weakness and Need – the character has a flaw that he needs to correct. Important: this weakness hurts other people as well as himself.
2. Desire – what the character actually wants, the story goal.
3. Opponent – the character competing with your character for the same goal.
4. Plan – the character must decide how he will get what he wants.
5. Battle – description of the point-counterpoint between character and opponent.
6. Self-revelation – character realizes his weakness and solves his need. He may or may not get his desire.
7. New equilibrium – the character's desire is gone, and he now works at a higher or lower emotional level.

Protagonist mirror subplots add depth and poignancy to the moral question you wrestle with in your book.

Exercise 61: Mirroring Subplots

Review your moral story pillar (Exercise 15) and your protagonist's hidden need (Exercise 24). Describe your protagonist's basic dilemma in a sentence. Are there more characters who could be grappling with the same root problem? Review your list of characters (Exercise 56). Could any of these be used for a subplot?

Free-write your thoughts. At the end, write down a sentence or two for each possible subplot.

Now, go through Truby's minimal list of story elements, and free-write how you might form a subplot. At the end, list what you might do for each step.

Exercise 62: Summary of Subplots

For this exercise, while your subplot ideas are still fresh in your mind, summarize them. For each strand record your notes and ideas for all of your possible story threads. Make sure you describe the purpose and progression of each one. You'll be using this subplot summary when you pull all of your story ideas together in the next level.

Chapter Nine

Comprehensive Template "Cheat Sheet"

The story structure is, for good or ill, fixed—although events and characters are infinitely varied, the deep flow or shape or bends of a story are remarkably consistent. By understanding and consciously using this innate structure, you will find shaping your own story much easier. You'll know what sorts of events and developments are needed at every stage, rather than blindly discovering these through tactile exploration.

This chapter takes an important pause for you to catch your breath before you move ahead to the next level by providing a valuable tool: a comprehensive review of the general structure of a story. When you're not sure what happens next as you summarize your story in the next level, use this template "cheat sheet," along with your unique ideas, to spark possibilities and to shape your story into something resonant and complete.

<u>Template "Cheat Sheet"</u>

A helpful way to organize your story if you find yourself stuck is to study the posts and general themes for each story quarter, and allow these to suggest goals, events, or character ideas. The following template tool is a comprehensive summary or "cheat sheet" of story structure. Remember that these statements are typical; I'm sure you can find story exceptions for some of these details, but the elements on the "cheat sheet" consistently appear. You won't go wrong by following this outline to the letter.

Character Role: (Pearson)

> Act One: Orphan
>
> Act Two/Part One: Wanderer
>
> Act Two/Part Two: Warrior
>
> Act Three: Martyr

Themes and Notes:

> Act One:
>
> - Sets up the story, introduces an invitation to change, then describes a delay until protagonist accepts the invitation.
> - Beware of using backstory.
>
> Act Two/Part One:
>
> - Acclimation to the new world, then three or four encounters with antagonists and/or contrasting themes with old world (present to past, alone to together, material to spiritual values, fear to faith, and so forth).
> - Protagonist meets new friends and allies who will go with him through the journey.
> - Tends to be a busy, positive section. There may be

threats, but protagonist handles them well using his old way of thinking.

- Purpose: showcase the new world. The protagonist learns the new world's rules.

- Protagonist has the sense (spoken or unspoken) that after these adventures, he will be able to go back to his ordinary world unchanged.

Act Two/Part Two:

- Three major themes: hidden need triplet; antagonists get stronger; and protagonist disintegrates.

- Generally the most difficult part of the story to write because this quarter is fragmented into many small narratives with intense scene weaving.

- Most variable part of the story structure-wise—but refer to this "cheat sheet" for confident structuring.

Act Three:

- Grand finale.

- Two parts: preparation for battle, and battle.

Story Strands:

Act One:

- B Strand (hidden need) and C Strand (antagonist) typically start within first three scenes.

- D Strand (gift at climax) and E Strand (protagonist's mirror) may begin during this quarter.

Act Two/Part One:

- B Strand (hidden need) not usually present on its own, although may be incorporated within another scene.

- C Strand (antagonist) has two or three brief

glimpses, often including the switch away beat (to be discussed in a moment).

- D Strand (gift at climax) may not have appeared yet. If present will only show a glimpse. May occasionally appear in switch away beat instead of C strand.

- E Strand (protagonist's mirror) not usually present on its own, although it may be incorporated within another scene.

Act Two/Part Two:

- intense subplot development and scene weaving.

- B Strand (hidden need) explores hidden need triplet.

- C Strand (antagonist) lines are profuse.

- D Strand (gift at climax) may start here if not before, and may be profuse.

- E Strand (protagonist's mirror) starts here if not before, and may be profuse. May end here or in act three.

Act Three:

- B Strand (hidden need) solution is demonstrated at the climax.

- There are sometimes two hidden needs: an outer and inner problem that grow from the same root. When this occurs one hidden need is solved in act two/part two, and the other at the climax. Film example: *Iron Will*.

- C Strand (antagonist) has interspersed scenes in first half of act, then merges with A strand (main story) in second half of act.

- D Strand (gift at climax) may have interspersed scenes in first half of act. This strand delivers around climax.

- E Strand (protagonist's mirror) is not usually present unless mixed with another strand.

Character Arc:

Establish protagonist identity—act one ordinary world.

Glimpse of core—act one argument.

Straddle identity and core—act two/part one.

Almost grasp core, but is afraid—act two/part two.

Protagonist decides to live core no matter what the consequences—act three climax.

Protagonist lives new life in core—act three resolution.

Story Structure:

Ordinary World (Act One)

- Shows the protagonist in his normal life, and often demonstrates a slow suffocation.
- Shows protagonist at home, at work, and at play (Snyder).
- Should be interesting to the reader even if the protagonist feels stifled.
- May involve a goal/mini-story of some sort (win argument, get somewhere on time).
- Protagonist is often the best at something (student, athlete, bum).

Inciting Incident (Story Post) (Act One)

- Often seems inconsequential at the time (offhand remark, found object).
- Invitation offered by inciting incident is not forced on protagonist—protagonist must choose to go this route.

Argument (Act One)

- Clear the deck of obstacles in preparation for accepting the invitation.

- External obstacles (for example, eliminate problems or make preparations).

- Internal obstacles (for example, make a decision to go forward).

- If protagonist's psychology would prevent him from choosing to accept the invitation, then your writer's job is to progressively remove all other options so that the protagonist must act.

Door (Story Post) (Act One)

- Final sequence of act one.

- Journey into the new world of act two.

- Length ranges from a few words to several scenes.

Switch Away Beat (Act Two/Part One)

- Occurs immediately after door.

- Usually follows a C story strand (antagonist) scene, although it may be a D story strand (gift at climax) scene.

- Purpose is to suspend tension after an exciting act one build-up by following an alternate story strand.

Acclimation Beat (Act Two/Part One)

- Occurs immediately after switch away beat.

- Purpose is to orient the reader or viewer to the new world of act two.

- Low key. The protagonist simply looks around and interacts a little, without anything happening.

Series of Encounters (Act Two/Part One)

- Usually three, or sometimes four, increasingly intense conflicts.
- Last conflict leads into midpoint.
- Conflicts can be against antagonist allies, against other opponents, and/or showcase events demonstrating changed themes from the old world (for example, present to past, alone to together, material to spiritual, fear to faith, etc.).
- Conflicts are not usually with the primary antagonist.
- Generally a positive section in which the protagonist is successful using his old way of thinking.

Booby Trap Encounter (Act Two/Part One)

- First encounter in series of encounters.
- Protagonist's first glimpse of forces against him.
- No direct contact.

A Step-Up Encounter (Act Two/Part One)

- Second encounter in series of encounters.
- More intense, more complex encounter.

Another Step-Up Encounter (Act Two/Part One)

- Third encounter in series of encounters.
- Even more intense, more complex encounter.
- May lead into midpoint.

Yet Another Step-Up Encounter (Act Two/Part One)

- Fourth encounter in series of encounters.
- Occasionally present.
- Intense.
- If present leads into midpoint.

Midpoint (Story Post) (Act Two/Part One)

- Often spectacular.

- After this point, the protagonist can no longer go back to his ordinary world unchanged.

- Two types of midpoint: disaster or false high.

Disaster Midpoint (Story Post) (Act Two/Part One)

- First of two types of story midpoint.

- Protagonist suffers devastating loss.

- Typically used when nature of climactic battle and/or primary antagonist is known in some sense to protagonist before the midpoint.

- Film example: *U571*.

False High Midpoint (Story Post) (Act Two/Part One)

- Second of two types of story midpoint.

- Protagonist seemingly conquers the new world using his old way of thinking.

- Typically used when nature of climactic battle and/or primary antagonist is not known in any sense to the protagonist until after the midpoint.

- In act two part one protagonist spends his time adjusting to an exotic new world and/or changed themes from old world.

- Film example: *Sky High*.

Hidden Need Triplet (Act Two/Part Two)

- Consists of three parts: hidden need is clearly demonstrated, hidden need is solved, and hidden need is demonstrated to be solved.

- These three parts may be presented together as a block or be woven with other story parts in the third quarter.

- Film example of block right after midpoint: *U571*.

Antagonists Get Stronger (Act Two/Part Two)

- C story strand, where all of the opponent forces gain strength.

- If story had a false high midpoint, primary antagonist is revealed in this quarter.

How Bad is the Antagonist Beat (Act Two/Part Two)

- Part of "antagonists get stronger" section of act two/part two. Normally occurs toward the end of this quarter.

- Shows antagonist doing his very worst to someone in a position that the protagonist may shortly find himself in also (mirror character). If the primary antagonist is a force, say a fire, this beat might show a devastating burn on a tract of land or person. If the primary antagonist is a person, he might torment another person or demonstrate potential damage he can inflict. Alternatively, the protagonist may simply experience a vision of astounding potential loss.

Protagonist Disintegrates (Act Two/Part Two)

- After midpoint protagonist is knocked for a loop.

- Protagonist fights and gathers clues to antagonist weakness and story problem. He continues to realize throughout this quarter that he is out of his element.

Slide (Story Post) (Act Two/Part Two)

- Can be spectacular, and is often devastating.

- There should be a death of some sort (person, dream, idea, place, etc.) (Snyder).

- Acts as an event funnel so that the specific nature of the final battle/climax is now clearly seen.

Preparation for Battle (Act Three)

- Protagonist knows that he can't beat the antagonist in a straight-on fight.

- Grim; protagonist gathers his resources, prepares to die, and develops a crazy plan as a strategy to use against the antagonist.

Crazy Plan (Act Three)

- Main focus of preparation for battle

- Unlikely plan to defeat the antagonist, but it could work if everything goes exactly right.

- It may be simple or elaborate.

Battle (Act Three)

- This is often the first time the protagonist and primary antagonist directly face off.

- There are usually at least three to six direct confrontations back to back.

- Protagonist may have a few victories, but in general loses ground.

- Stereotyped final sequence of last battle: darkest moment, help from outside, climax, and resolution.

Darkest Moment (Story Post) (Act Three)

- Protagonist is spent and ready to die.

- Protagonist may experience worse consequences than previously thought. For example, the protagonist realizes that not only will he die, but others will die because he failed.

- Often includes a sacrificial act.

Help from Outside (Story Post) (Act Three)

- This is a small action, memory, or circumstance that doesn't cause a win, but gives hope and strength for the protagonist to try one more time.

Climax (Story Post) (Act Three)

- Through the protagonist's efforts, crazy plan, and/or gift at climax subplot (strand D), the protagonist usually decisively wins the confrontation.

- The protagonist occasionally loses the final confrontation, although this is a less popular outcome with audience.

- Protagonist may lose but have compensatory victory. Film example: *Rocky*.

Resolution (Story Post) (Act Three)

- Demonstrates how life will go on now that the story problem has been solved.

- Occasionally contains a "fillip:" a piece of information or situation at the very end that ties ends together unexpectedly or changes the interpretation of what went before. Novel example: *A Shortcut in Time* by Charles Dickinson.

Conclusion

Despite this detailed structure, writing a novel or screenplay is not a formula. I like to think of the story as being the rigid frame, whereas the unique events, settings, characters, and writing style/vision make the story into art.

Some people have trouble believing that the story is as rigid as is represented here. All I can say is that I've collected and tabulated the data, and this description is sound. Even though it may seem counterintuitive to use such a detailed checklist, I promise to you that if you follow this outline, your story will be proportional, complete, and original with your own ideas and writing style.

LEVEL FIVE:

Integration

You are now on the fifth level of story construction. This is the transition level from general story to breaking it down into scenes: from the dreaming, or the abstract, into the concrete nuts-and-bolts of storytelling. This level is challenging because for the first time you'll be integrating your thoughts and dreams into a coherent, consistent narrative that someone else can follow. You've generated an enormous amount of material, and probably have some amazing and unexpected directions in which you'd like to take your story. And maybe you feel a little overwhelmed with how it all fits together? Not to worry. This level will help you organize everything you have into a single whole that you can use to start actually writing the story.

Chapter Ten

Synopsis

Now that you've thought through your story several times, it's time to write the events up into two summaries: the 200-word pitch, and the classic three to five page double-spaced synopsis. You may also wish to write an extra-long double-spaced summary (five or more pages), with all of your writer's notes for execution etc., simply as a reminder aid for yourself if you feel this is helpful. These synopses will be for your eyes only at this point, but you'll eventually want to polish them as part of the submission package for your book or screenplay when you start looking for an agent. If you are writing a screenplay, for submission you'll also need to develop a treatment of about twenty-five pages in which you describe each scene in miniature. I won't discuss preparing this document, but I briefly review submission details in Chapter Seventeen. You can also review the listed resources in Appendix One for more help.

The pitch is written to intrigue, but your longer synopsis should contain "spoilers" (information that gives away your story's ideas), including the ending. This is because agents and editors need to quickly grasp your story and don't have time to read the entire manuscript or screenplay, at least until you get further along with them in the process. In your synopsis avoid flowery descriptions, stunning dialogue, and lengthy explanations or character descriptions. One other point: no matter which tense and point of view you use in your story (to be discussed in Chapter Fifteen), these documents are written in present tense third person. I don't know why.

I prefer to start by writing the pitch of about 200 words. This is a longer version of your logline, and helpful for selling your book, say in a query letter. I then move to the longer, or classic, synopsis—telling the story in ten to fifteen or so paragraphs (three to five pages). If you find yourself writing more, you may wish to convert this into your extra-long, or kitchen sink, synopsis, then edit a copy down to the classic version. Once I have the classic document, I will occasionally edit it down into a third synopsis: a one-page (single-spaced) or two-page (double-spaced) short synopsis. You can find examples of pitches for *Dracula* and *The Count of Monte Cristo* in this chapter, and classic synopses for these books in Appendix Two at the back of the book.

Pitch

There is no "one way" to write the pitch. I suggest you study the backs of book covers to get a sense of what these might be like. The purpose of the pitch is to give a brief description of your story so the reader feels compelled to learn more.

I have a general formula I use for my own pitches, although these suggestions are flexible and not hard-and-fast rules. If you'd like, you can follow along with me.

At the top of the page, write your fifteen to twenty word logline that describes your story.

Next, write an intriguing set-up of your problem or inciting incident in two to four sentences.

Next, write some of the problems that occur during the beginning-middle of the story in two or three sentences.

Next, hint at the deeper problems of your story in one or two sentences.

Finally, end the pitch on a one sentence cliff-hanger.

Here are 2 examples:

DRACULA: (212 words)

An unlikely group of professionals and friends discovers a mythical evil that is surprisingly real and determined to infiltrate 1900s England.

A young English solicitor, Jonathan Harker, travels to Eastern Europe to do business with a Transylvanian noble. Although the local people urge Harker not to proceed, and one woman even hangs a crucifix about his neck, he enters the mysterious castle of Count Dracula. Soon he learns his host climbs walls like a bat, has no reflection in a mirror, and will not let him go. Three dreamlike women hunt him and almost steal his soul; he fears he will go mad.

Harker escapes to England and rejoins his five friends, only to find the dear friend of his fiancée dying from a mysterious wasting illness. A learned professor, Van Helsing, recognizes the unusual symptoms. Further educated by Harker's observations of his terrifying ordeal, Van Helsing leads the hunt to extinguish the vampire Dracula before the Count can wreak more damage. Dracula has more influence and cunning than expected, though, and soon establishes a strong presence in England. As the group of friends helplessly watch, Harker's fiancée falls ill with the same symptoms that killed her friend. Can the small band of vampire hunters stake Dracula before he kills them all?

THE COUNT OF MONTE CRISTO: (190 words)

A wrongfully-imprisoned young man gains freedom and a fortune that he uses to wreak an elaborate revenge.

This story takes place in the grand sweep of Napoleonic France. Nineteen-year-old sailor Edmond Dantès has just been promoted to ship's captain, and plans to marry his great love in a few days. Unfortunately dangerous jealousy stirs the hearts of three of his so-called friends who conspire to accuse him of treason. Edmond is thrown into a rocky prison in which he almost goes mad from isolation until he meets a fellow prisoner tunneling under his cell. This prisoner teaches Edmond all he knows, including the location of an unimaginable fortune that Edmond believes may be fantasy.

When the prisoner dies, Edmond sews himself into the man's shroud and escapes to find the treasure, then Edmond's erstwhile companions who imprisoned him for years.

With his wealth and disguises, Edmond becomes dangerous as he righteously rewards or ruins one man after another, bringing long-hidden secrets to light. Edmond's plans are elaborate and unexpectedly fitting, but as his revenge leaves a trail of devastation, he begins to wonder if forgiveness is more powerful than anger.

Exercise 63: Pitch

Write out your pitch.

Classic Synopsis

The synopsis gives the essence of your story—plot high points, character thumbnails, story world, moral lesson—in an entertaining fashion. It focuses on the main story. Subplots may be hinted, but there isn't enough room to fully explore them.

As you write your synopsis, remember that you can change things if you don't like them, so just write. Aim for about ten to fifteen paragraphs. If you find yourself writing more, just finish up your synopsis, then make a copy and edit that one down.

If you're stuck, tell your story out loud to a friend or yourself. Review your plot points and the essence of your story. Study examples of synopses. A terrific resource to help with writing synopses is *Writing the Fiction Synopsis* by Pam McCutcheon.

Here are some exercises to clarify your thoughts before actually starting the writing.

Exercise 64: Preliminary Story Structure
Repeat Exercise 20.

Exercise 65: General Events
List the general events that occur in your story.

Exercise 66: Characters
Review Exercises 56 and 57, then list your characters. Choose the main characters central to your plot, and identify their goals, motivations, and conflicts.

Exercise 67: Setting
Review Exercise 11. In a concise paragraph, describe your setting, especially focusing on the unique, "gee whiz" aspects.

Exercise 68: Subplots

Review Exercise 62, then list the subplots of your story. Identify each as hidden need (B strand), antagonist (C strand), gift at climax (D strand) and/or protagonist's mirror (E strand). Recognize that for your synopsis, you will probably only include the high points of the B, C, and D strands. E strand may come in if the actions of E's main character impinge on the other strands.

Exercise 69: Theme

Review Exercise 15. What is the theme of your story: the take-home message you want to convey to your reader or viewer? Write it in a single sentence. Review Exercises 24, 39, and 58. Describe what your protagonist learns during the story (his hidden need).

You should now have a good general idea of your story. It's time to just dive in and write your synopsis.

Chapter Eleven

Bubbles and Reveals

Bubbles

The "bubble" is my shorthand term for a sequence of about one to six scenes describing a larger action within the story. In screenwriting jargon what I call bubbles are sometimes called "beats." Each bubble has an author purpose, a theme, and a location. The bubble is the intermediate unit for planning your story, allowing you to go from a general sense of how you want your story to flow to specific conflicts and settings that will actually demonstrate your story to your audience.

Each bubble takes place in a different location. When the location changes, so does the bubble. The location is general, so, for example, if part of the story takes place in the living room and then the kitchen, this would probably be considered one bubble, although it could be two if you have a constricted story world and incorporate a sharp delineation of events.

Here is an example of six bubbles that span between act one and act two/part one from the film *The Fellowship of the Ring*, starting a bit after the beginning of the story. I chose this section because the bubbles are distinct, with no scene weaving.

Bubble A

Location: Frodo's house in the Shire.

Theme: Danger is about to descend onto Middle Earth.

Author Purpose: Inciting Incident to establish the story goal.

Summary: Gandalf tells Frodo that he must travel to Mordor to destroy the One Ring, and Frodo and Sam resolve to journey to do this.

Story Strand: A

Bubble B

Location: Montage of traveling, and finally a field along the outskirts of the Shire.

Theme: Door or journey into the new world.

Author Purpose: Protagonist accepts the challenge to enter the new world.

Summary: In a field, Sam tells Frodo if he takes one more step, he'll be further from the Shire than he's ever been. They walk forward.

Story Strand: A

Bubble C

Location: Castle of Isengard

Theme: Betrayal of a friend/ally (Saruman) to evil side.

Author Purpose: switch away beat: reminder that opponent is active. (Secondary opponent, Saruman, is working to do the will of the primary opponent, Sauron).

Summary: Gandalf travels to ask counsel of his teacher Saruman about the Ring. He learns that the Nazgûl have left to find Frodo and the Ring, and that Saruman is working for Sauron. Gandalf is captured.

Story Strand: C

Bubble D

Location: Farmer Maggot's garden.

Theme: Acclimation to the new world beat.

Author Purpose: Protagonist meets new friends to help in the journey.

Summary: Frodo and Sam meet Merry and Pippin, and they romp in Farmer Maggot's garden. The hobbits look for mushrooms, then fall down a hill onto a road.

Story Strand: A

Bubble E

Location: Road.

Theme: Protagonist's first encounter with opponent. (Secondary opponents, the Nazgûl, are working to do the will of the primary opponent, Sauron).

Author Purpose: Booby Trap Encounter—no actual contact, but protagonist gets his first glimpse of opponent.

Summary: While the other hobbits explore the road Frodo senses a vague danger and hurries the hobbits to hide within the roots of a giant tree. The Nazgûl ride up behind the tree but don't find them. Another encounter occurs on the road a few hours later, but the hobbits eventually escape by jumping over water onto a raft.

Story Strand: A, C

Bubble F

Location: Town of Bree.

Theme: Protagonist's second encounter with opponent. (The secondary opponents, the Nazgûl, are working to do the will of the primary opponent, Sauron).

Author Purpose: Protagonist meets another friend for the journey who is a key player in both the D (gift at climax) and E (protagonist's mirror) story strands. In the outer D story strand subplot, Aragorn is instrumental in clearing many opponents to save Frodo, both in this movie and the two sequels. In the inner E story strand subplot, Aragorn is a mirror character to protagonist Frodo because his righteous need to take up power (regain his rightful kingship as heir of Gondor) contrasts with Frodo's righteous need to discard power (destroy the One Ring).

Summary: The hobbits travel to the town of Bree where they had arranged to meet with Gandalf. However Gandalf has not kept the appointment because he is being held captive by Saruman. In the tavern, Frodo puts on the One Ring, and the Nazgûl learn where he is. They break into Bree. The hobbits meet Strider (Aragorn) who saves them from the Nazgûl.

Story Strand: A, C, D, E

And so forth.

Reveals

A reveal is a shorthand notation of a single action. Reveals are another useful tool, along with bubbles, to diagram how a story flows. Each reveal is put in the form of: character action/goal → BUT an obstacle.

Here is a reveal sequence for the above bubble sequence:

Frodo wants to hide the ring → BUT Gandalf says it must be returned to Mordor.

Frodo will go alone → BUT Gandalf finds Sam and tells him to go with Frodo.

Frodo and Sam travel in the Shire → BUT they cross the barrier to new world.

Gandalf goes for advice from Saruman → BUT Saruman is a traitor and captures him.

Frodo and Sam seem lost in field → BUT they find Merry and Pippin, and they all romp.

The hobbits find mushrooms on the road → BUT Frodo suspects danger and they hide.

The Nazgûl come close to capturing the hobbits on the road → BUT the hobbits escape.

The hobbits arrive in the walled town of Bree to meet Gandalf → BUT Gandalf has not arrived.

Frodo puts on the One Ring → BUT the Nazgûl now know where he is.

Aragorn (Strider) observes Frodo put on the Ring and takes him away to question him → BUT he saves Frodo and the hobbits from the Nazgûl who break into Bree.

Writing Your Bubbles and Reveals

Writing bubbles and reveals may be the most difficult part of structuring your story so far because this is the first time you're going from beginning to end in detail. It may take some thought and trial-and-error over a few days or even longer to get a satisfactory event sequence. Don't worry about it—just put something down, and go back and change or adapt as ideas occur to you. When you're finished, this set of bubbles and reveals could be an adequate outline for you to write your story. However, if you're uncomfortable to hear this you'll be happy to learn that we will add one more safety net, with the story board process in the next chapter, before writing commences.

Like the synopsis, the best way to write your bubbles and reveals is just to write them. Put in the ones you know, and then go back to fill in the gaps. Use the clues about your story that you've already generated in the last chapter, along with the comprehensive review of the template ("cheat sheet") to spark ideas in forming your complete story.

The number of bubbles (location changes) is fairly consistent: in general at least seven, and no more than ten, in each story quarter.

Exercise 70: Writing Bubbles
Split your story into four quarters and list your bubble sequence.

Exercise 71: Series of Reveals
Break up your bubbles into reveal notation. Make a statement of the goal or action, do an arrow, and then a BUT: Harry wants to find the paper → BUT he learns that Joe has taken it home. This process will give you a linked flow of events through your story.

Summary

And there you go. These bubbles and reveals organize and arrange your story events. You should have about twenty-eight to forty bubbles when you're finished, and a reveal sequence that expands upon your bubble events.

Chapter Twelve

Story Boarding

Story Boarding

Story boarding is a popular technique especially used by screen-writers to plan a story, but useful for any type of story writer. It's time to break out your index cards. You also need a large space—the dining room table, the floor, or for a more permanent location you might use a large corkboard with push pins. Alternatively, if you have an available wall that can withstand masking tape, you may want to use this. We will call this space the "frame."

Exercise 72: Set up Story Board Frame

Gather your materials and set up your workspace for story boarding. With masking tape mark out four long horizontal strips on your frame to separate the acts.

If you're writing a screenplay, you'll aim for ten scenes (cards) in each quarter, for a total of forty scenes. If you're writing a novel, you'll aim for at least ten, and up to fifteen

> *to twenty scenes, per quarter giving a maximum of sixty to eighty scenes. Each of your bubbles normally breaks down to about one to three scenes, up to a maximum of about six.*

Writing the Scenes

In this chapter you'll develop a first approximation for how your story might unfold scene-wise. You will almost certainly make multiple changes to the sequence as you start writing your story, so for now just put something down. When in doubt, record your ideas because you have plenty of time to polish later.

For each scene card, put down the 5W's and H of journalistic reporting: why, who, what, when, where, how. Let's go over each of these categories:

Why

Why are you, the author, including this scene? There must be a good reason.

Who

Unless you're writing a novel in first person, your story will be told from the rotating viewpoints of various characters. I touch upon point of view (POV) in Chapter Fifteen, but for now just write down who you think is the most impacted character in this scene to tell it.

What

What is the character's goal? What are the beginning and end points, or positions, of this scene?

When

When in the story does this scene take place?

Where

Where does this scene take place?

How

How does this scene unfold? Include as many internal and external obstacles as you can.

Indicate at the top of your card whether this scene is tending more toward hopeful (positive) or desperate (negative). A good rule of thumb is to line up your scenes in alternating order: positive-negative-positive-negative-positive and so forth.

Exercise 73: Subplot Cards

Pull out your subplot summary sheet that you wrote a few chapters ago (Exercise 62). Now break each subplot down into the series of actions that will complete the story. Review Truby's seven stages of a story arc (weakness/need, desire, opponent, plan, battle, self-revelation, new equilibrium) in Chapter Eight if you need to, especially for your E strand mirror subplot(s). Remember that not every subplot needs a story arc.

Using your list, break your subplots into scenes and write one scene per card. Mark each card with the story strand(s) it covers. Put these cards aside.

Exercise 74: Story Post Cards

On a separate card for each, write down your story posts as a scene (Inciting Incident, Door, Midpoint, Slide, Darkest Moment, Help from Outside, Climax, Resolution). Tape or pin these in approximately the correct place within your frame: For example, the inciting incident is about halfway through act one, the door is at the end of act one, and so forth. Use the diagram in Chapter Five if you need to refresh your memory of what goes where.

For the remaining exercises in this chapter, use the template "cheat sheet" and your notes to spark ideas for scenes. Write as many cards as you want for each section; you'll be able to combine or eliminate later.

Exercise 75: Ordinary World Cards

Stories should start with a hook (see Chapter Thirteen).

The ordinary world shows the protagonist "at home, at work, and at play" (Snyder). Include a scene demonstrating the protagonist's hidden need, and possibly one showing the antagonist.

Determine which subplot cards may go in this section.

Complete at least five cards that can go before the inciting incident, preferably seven or more if you're writing a novel.

Exercise 76: Argument Cards

Study your inciting incident card to identify any changes you might want to make based on your ordinary world. Identify the bridging goal.

For the argument, write about goal pursuit and/or internal and external obstacles that prevent the protagonist from pursing the inciting incident's invitation.

Determine which subplot cards may go in this section.

Complete at least five cards that can go after the inciting incident, preferably seven or more if you're writing a novel.

Exercise 77: Act Two/Part One Cards

Study your door card to identify any changes you might want to make based on your act one.

This second story quarter is usually comprised of three or four, increasingly intense, general action sequences. Themes are dealing with opponents and/or dealing with the new world.

Determine which subplot cards may go in this section (very few!).

Complete at least ten cards, preferably twelve to fifteen if you're writing a novel.

Exercise 78: Act Two/Part Two Cards

Study your midpoint card to identify any changes you might want to make based on your previous work. Is this a false high or a disaster midpoint?

This third story quarter is made of many small narratives that are woven together. These themes include hidden need triplet, antagonists get stronger, and protagonist disintegrates. Furthermore, subplots are profuse in this section.

Determine which subplot cards may go in this section.

Complete at least ten cards, preferably twelve to fifteen if you're writing a novel.

Exercise 79: Preparation for Battle Cards

Study your slide card to identify any changes you might want to make based on your previous work. Make sure there is a physical death and/or death of an idea in the slide.

Themes explored in this preparation for battle section are the protagonist's development of a crazy plan and the antagonist's making preparations for the upcoming battle.

Determine which subplot cards may go in this section.

Complete at least five cards, preferably seven or more if you're writing a novel.

Exercise 80: Battle Cards

This section is the equivalent of the fireworks finale at the 4th of July. The protagonist and primary antagonist directly engage. There are often three to six battles, each more intense than before. Finally, the story ends with the stereotyped sequence of darkest moment, help from outside, climax, resolution. Study these story post cards to identify any changes you might want to make based on your previous work. Consider including a fillip in your story.

Determine which subplot cards may go in this section. If they haven't already ended, subplots must also end here. Tie them off from least to most important.

Complete at least five cards, preferably seven or more if you're writing a novel.

Exercise 81: Overview Cards

Study your cards. Talk through your story scene by scene and rearrange, add, or subtract cards as appropriate. If you have fewer than ten cards in any quarter, fill those holes. Make your story a consistent narrative from beginning to end.

Excellent work! Story boarding is intense but helpful for visualizing the flow of your story. Once you're happy with your scene content and order, place your cards into a stable form, either leaving them on the frame if you can, or else binding them in a binder, box, or with a rubber band. Keep them available for Level Six where you'll begin the writing process.

LEVEL SIX:

Genesis

You are now on the sixth level of story construction. On this level you'll investigate some writing techniques, and start putting words down for your first draft. At the end of this level you'll have a first approximation of how, exactly, you can work from your outline to write your manuscript.

Chapter Thirteen

Beginnings

Start your story by intriguing your reader. He may not stay with you for more than a few pages in your book or screenplay unless he becomes interested.

Write your scenes in a logical progression of revelation without including irrelevant detail. Don't show your characters just sitting and thinking. They should always be doing something.

Let's take a look at specific tools you can use to open well:

Setting

Screenplays automatically establish setting, but in novels settings must be built. Your reader needs concrete markers to understand the context of what he's reading. At the same time, you don't want to include so much information that it distracts from the story. Be efficient with your language—don't stop the action to describe the scene, but throw in context through the dialogue and action. For example, if you mention that your protagonist while walking in a garden hears a car beep, the reader can deduce that he's probably near the road or a driveway. Other context clues will solidify this.

Describe your protagonist's internal reactions to the setting, not just the outer details.

Exercise 82: Opening Setting

Where might your book or screenplay open? What sort of sense or feeling is conveyed in the opening image: peaceful, claustrophobic, chaotic, or something else? Are there any other settings you might consider in which to open your story? What is your character doing in this setting besides looking around? What does he think of this setting? If you only stood aside to watch your character, what would you learn about him?

Dialogue

Dialogue is a useful tool to convey information without breaking away from the story, and a great way to open your story, providing your characters have something to say. Avoid mundane statements (Hello, How are you?). Dialogue is covered in more detail in Chapter Fifteen.

Avoid Extraneous Information

Information that isn't directly relevant to the story action at hand, such as back story or introspection by your characters while they drink tea, will kill your story. Only include immediately essential information.

Don't Follow Too Many Characters

When opening a story, remaining with one character for a few scenes builds reader engagement. Introduce characters one at a time so that the reader can meet them without becoming confused.

Exercise 83: Opening Character

Who will first appear in your story? Why? Is your opening character your protagonist? What is your opening character trying to accomplish? Who else is there? How will you make your opening character interesting?

An Intriguing Situation

Above all, you must interest your reader within the first few pages.

The most direct way to do this is by establishing an appealing, ambiguous, or otherwise provocative opening situation—something at least a little odd that causes the reader to pay attention. Even if you focus your story around an unusual character rather than action, you must show a situation that demonstrates why he is interesting.

The situation should do at least one, and preferably more, of the following three things:

1. Make your audience curious (not confused) about what's going on.
2. Raise interesting questions.
3. Tap into an emotion.

Many stories start with a disruption that knocks the ordinary world off balance, followed by the inciting incident later in act one. For example, the film *Witness* opens with Amish life as a little boy and his mother prepare for a journey. In a Philadelphia train station the little boy witnesses a murder which disrupts the ordinary world. However, the protagonist isn't the little boy but John, the policeman. The inciting incident occurs when the little boy recognizes a police official as the murderer, and John realizes he must make the decision to go after the official.

You may wish to use this disruption technique of the ordinary world to start your story.

Exercise 84: Opening Situation

Describe what is going on as you open your story. Will the situation be immediately obvious to an observer, and/or are you able to explain it in a few sentences and without backstory? What questions might this situation raise in the reader's mind? Will you open with an event that disturbs the ordinary world in some way?

Some Thoughts about Opening with a Bang

Some writers espouse opening a story that sets the reader or viewer immediately into the middle of a horrific disaster or other spectacular event. While this can work well, especially for films, this is a challenging technique to pull off especially for new writers.

Before the reader can be drawn into the disaster, he needs to understand what is going on (clearly presented descriptions and detail) and to care about the characters. A horrific unfolding disaster may even prevent the reader's emotional engagement into your story because it's so painful that he won't want to become involved.

I would like to suggest, instead of a devastating situation, that you form a relationship between your reader and point of view character. If you must have the exciting fire or other big event, build into it and allow the time for your reader and character to first become acquainted.

Building a Relationship Between Your Reader and Your Protagonist

Building reader interest in your protagonist can be done in several ways:

Create Sympathy

If your protagonist suffers from something, whether an injustice, a physical defect, or a terrible loss of some sort, this will go a long way to create reader identification because the reader will feel sorry for him and therefore, of course, want him to win.

Put Your Protagonist in Jeopardy

Any time a character is in real danger, whether by physical or emotional threat, the audience is riveted. Start with a jeopardy small enough so the reader doesn't automatically disengage from a painful situation, and build up from there.

Make Your Protagonist Likeable

We all want to be around pleasant rather than unpleasant people, and this is no different in stories. The person may behave well, or be funny, or be good at his job, or whatever—he has likeable traits that the viewer can appreciate.

Exercise 85: Opening Character

Why should the reader care about your opening character? Is he an individual and distinguishable from another person who might be put into his position? How?

Create an Immediate External Short-Term Goal

Make clear to your reader who your protagonist is and what they're rooting for him to do in the first few pages. To add tension, you can always throw in a ticking clock. For example, your hero might have to deliver something by five o'clock and keeps being slowed by obstacles.

Exercise 86: Opening Scene

Review Exercises 82 through 85. Summarize your thoughts for how you might want to open your story. Can you think of alternative scenarios? Can you include a time limit or ticking clock of some sort? What message do you want to communicate to the reader after he reads your first scene? How can you communicate this?

The Opening Line

Finally, for preplanning your first scene you need to craft a compelling opening line. One of my favorite techniques is to write a sentence full of irony or suggestive of an intriguing character or situation.

Exercise 87: Opening Line

Read the examples of opening lines in Appendix Three, and then imagine what your first line might be. Write at least five, try them out on your friends, and modify as appropriate.

Chapter Fourteen

Writing the Individual Scene

The scene is the basic unit of the story. There are normally about forty scenes in a screenplay and up to sixty or eighty scenes in a novel.

In many newbie manuscripts that I've critiqued, and even some published books, there may be a lot of action but I find I can't always identify how this scene pushes the story ahead. I'll find myself thinking, Who are these people? What is at stake? Why should I care?

This chapter will review how to plan each scene so you don't run into this problem. For the least amount of writing frustration and for a shapely story, I recommend you repeat this process of scene planning for each scene before you dive in to write.

Once you plan your scene, write it in draft form while your ideas and enthusiasm are fresh. Then, and only then, should you start to work on the next scene. Don't worry if your words aren't perfect because that's what editing and a second draft are for. (See Chapter Sixteen on editing).

This sequence of exercises will bring clarity to your scenes, and help to prevent the common newbie problem of unfocused writing.

Just like you did for story boarding (Chapter Twelve), you need to answer the five W's and H of the scene, this time in closer detail in preparation for writing. Let's go through these:

Exercise 88: Scene Why

WHY: If you took this scene out, would your story collapse? Describe why you, the author, need to include this scene in your story. What function(s) will it serve? What needs to happen? Are there other scenes that could fulfill this purpose? If you can, take it out.

Exercise 89: Scene Who

WHO: Who absolutely must be in this scene? Who doesn't need to be there? Keep your scene guest list as small as possible to avoid reader confusion.

Exercise 90: Scene Who 2

WHO: Through whose eyes will you be telling this scene (point of view (POV) discussed in Chapter Fifteen)? Usually this POV character is chosen because he is most affected by events in the scene, and/or the one who can give the best insight through his thoughts of what these events might mean.

Exercise 91: Scene What

WHAT: As the author, explain the purpose of this scene. What are the goals of each character? What are the stakes? What is the scene question? What happens in this scene? What obstacles (internal and external) will your protagonist face? Try to list at least two or three.

Exercise 92: Scene When

WHEN: How soon after the last scene is this one taking place? What events happened prior to this scene? What time of day will it take place?

Exercise 93: Scene Where

WHERE: Where will this scene take place? Describe the setting and list some non-stereotyped details to include in your draft. Can the setting somehow contribute to plot, character, or moral revelations? How does your POV character respond to the setting? Now, imagine two or three different (surprising) settings in which this scene might take place. Does one of these settings make the scene more interesting? For example, in the film Rocky, *Rocky's first date with Adrienne in a skating rink is more memorable than it would have been in a restaurant.*

Exercise 94: Scene How

HOW: How will this scene unfold? Will it be generally positive or negative? Remember from Chapter Twelve that stories can benefit from a scene sequence that alternates positives and negatives. What unexpected events might occur? For example, as your protagonist is arguing with someone, a car may crash through the window. Can you brainstorm at least three different ways in which this scene may occur?

Exercise 95: Scene Summary

Close your eyes and imagine your scene unfold. When you've got a part or the whole that seems good, take notes to remember the dialogue and sequence of events that occurred. Write down anything striking that you wish to remember for writing your draft. Determine what the POV character's situation is at the beginning of the scene, and what it is at the end.

A Specialized Writing Technique for the Novel

For the novel, Dwight Swain (*Techniques of the Selling Author*), Jack Bickham (*Elements of Writing Fiction: Scene and Structure*), and others have suggested that there are two general types of scenes: Scenes, with a capital "S," and Sequels.

Roughly speaking, the Scene follows the external advancing plot, and the Sequel describes the internal, POV character's reactions to each development. Stories are then composed of beads of Scene-Sequel-Scene-Sequel. The Scenes push the action forward and increase the speed of the story, whereas the Sequels slow it down. To speed up a plodding manuscript, simply shorten your Sequels to a paragraph or even a single sentence before moving into the next Scene. If your manuscript is moving too quickly, lengthen your Sequels. However don't eliminate either Scenes or Sequels since the story depends on developing both of these external and internal story lines.

The Scene and the Sequel both have important elements that you need to decide upon before starting to write.

While the advice in this chapter applies to complete Scenes and Sequels, this principle translates to smaller units showing a single action and then the character's reaction to it. The back-and-forth on this small level segues into the writing technique of the MRU (motivation-reaction unit) that is discussed in Chapter Fifteen.

The Scene

The Scene focuses on the external action of the plot—what a camera would capture if it were filming your story. I've found it helpful to paste the following outline to the top of the page and fill it in before starting:

POV:

GOAL:

CONFLICT:

DISASTER:

POV:

POV stands for the point of view character, the character in whose head you will be writing from. I talk more about POV in Chapter Fifteen. Generally speaking, the POV character is the person most affected by the events of this scene, and/or whose opinions and thoughts will be most helpful for the reader. If you write in a different voice than third person limited, this category may not be relevant.

Exercise 96: Scene POV

From whose POV is this Scene told? Could anyone else tell it? What would each character be able to add to the understanding of this Scene?

GOAL:

Before you start, take a few moments to understand what each character desires in this Scene.

Start the draft of your Scene by clearly stating at the beginning (or at the end of the previous sequence leading to this Scene), in one clear sentence, the POV character's goal. This should be something that can be answered with a yes or no. Something like, *"William knew he needed to find the box before Tommy did, and he only had a five minute head start."* Although your reader probably won't be aware of what you're doing with this sentence, your clear statement focuses him to understand what he should be watching for within the action, and will allow him to sense, at the end, whether the Scene goal was met or not.

Exercise 97: Scene Goal

What is your POV character's goal for this Scene? Can its attainment be answered with a clear, yes-or-no answer? Can you state this goal in one clear sentence that you can use for your draft?

CONFLICT:

The conflict comprises the largest proportion of your Scene, and is what makes it exciting. The essence of the conflict is the series of obstacles that prevent the POV character from just waltzing through to attain his goal.

Obstacles are both external (other people, physical barriers) and internal (fears, worries, lack of knowledge). For preplanning your scene, you should attempt to list at least five. Even if you don't use all of these obstacles while writing your draft, they are helpful to prevent writer's block—if you become stuck while writing, just introduce another problem.

Exercise 98: Scene Conflict

List as many obstacles to your POV character's achieving his Scene goal as you can. Then list a sequence of the point-counterpoint exchange that could occur in your Scene from beginning to end. Imagine some surprises: for example, a character suddenly appearing halfway through.

DISASTER:

The disaster is how the Scene ends. Unless your POV character is the antagonist, most of the time you should put your POV character in a worse situation at the end of the Scene than he was at the beginning. Minimally, make the ending ambivalent— the protagonist achieves his Scene goal, but he has sustained a loss and/or is aware of much more to accomplish before the end of the story. More questions are raised! The reader thinks, *I'll read just one more chapter...*

If your POV character is your antagonist, then in general he should be successful with his Scene goals, and also be in a better position at the end of the Scene than he was at the beginning.

The Disaster (or Scene end) can finish in four ways:

<u>Yes</u>: The POV character achieves his goal. Since it stops the story action, I recommend only using this with good reason.

<u>Yes, But</u>: The POV character achieves his goal, but also gains more problems. For example, let's say that Jim's Scene goal is to ask his boss for a raise. The boss might say, sure, but you'll have to work an extra ten hours a week. This is an effective ending.

<u>No</u>: The POV character does not achieve his goal. For example, Jim's boss says no to the raise. A "No" Scene can be removed from the story without harm since it doesn't advance the forward action—the protagonist is in the same position at the beginning and end of the Scene.

<u>No, and Furthermore</u>: The POV character does not achieve his goal, and furthermore he gains more problems. For example, Jim's boss says no to the raise, and furthermore fires Jim. This is an effective ending.

Exercise 99: Scene Disaster

How will your Scene end? How will your POV character's situation be changed from the beginning?

The Sequel

The Sequel focuses on the internal portion of your plot and draws the reader in so he cares about your characters and your story. The ability to directly convey thought and emotion is perhaps the biggest advantage the novel has over the screenplay. The screenplay, of course, has its own set of advantages such as the ability to create an overwhelming multisensory experience.

Sequels are often neglected simply because they're easy to neglect. They're quiet and not demanding. The writer might be so intent upon working out elaborate plot twists that he forgets the reader's need to bond with the characters.

Sequels slow down the story's action. Occasionally during an intensely active portion of the plot the writer can get away with skipping the Sequel, but this should happen infrequently. The Sequel is often short, on the order of a paragraph or two, and can be tacked onto the end of a Scene rather than have its own section.

Sequels describe the POV character's internal response to the disaster of the previous scene. I've found it helpful to paste the following outline to the top of the page and fill it out before starting:

EMOTION:
THOUGHT:
DECISION:
ACTION:

This order is logical and easy to remember. When faced with a shocking or devastating event, the person is first overcome with emotion—fear, rage, or sadness. Next, he begins to process what this event might mean and possible actions he can take. Then, he makes a decision for his next goal. Finally, he starts to accomplish this goal. The goal is carried over and begins the next Scene.

Exercise 100: Scene Emotion

Restate the disaster that occurred in the previous Scene. What will be the POV character's emotional reaction to this?

Exercise 101: Scene Thought

How will the POV character process this information? What will be the most important implication to him? What alternatives might he imagine to deal with his new circumstances?

Exercise 102: Scene Decision

What action will the POV character decide to take? Remember that the most poignant decisions are based on a Dilemma: a choice between two (or more) bad alternatives. When you write the draft, lay out explicitly why each alternative is bad, and then explain the POV character's reasoning for choosing the one he does.

Exercise 103: Next Action

This section can sometimes be implied rather than shown. It demonstrates that the POV character is moving to enact his decision.

There is no easy way to write your first draft, but doing this little bit of scene preplanning is helpful to prevent writers block. As you write, you may find scenes going in a different direction than you'd originally planned, but it's okay to go with the flow. At the end, analyze your scene to make sure it does what you, the author, need it to do. If it doesn't work for whatever reasons, just go back to your notes and start again.

Chapter Fifteen

Writing Techniques

Overview

Many techniques exist for writers to make their stories real and immediate to readers. This chapter touches upon a few concepts of which you should be aware so that you can focus your attention on their mastery. The only way to get good at the actual writing is to practice. I recommend that after reading this chapter you find technique writing books (see Appendix One) to expand your understanding of these things as you begin work on your draft.

Showing Not Telling

This chestnut holds much truth, and means that a story is shown in scenes, not in narrative summary or character reflection. Although a screenplay is not as prone to this problem as a novel, beware of information dumps in dialogue.

For a novel you should imagine how a scene would appear if you filmed it. For instance, a girl jumping off her bicycle, running to the backyard, and sitting in a tree for ten minutes while she thinks is dull. Can you have the girl pursue a scene goal as discussed in Chapter Fourteen? If she needs to reflect, can you show her pulling apart a flower as she decides on a course of action, or conversing with someone to explain her worries? To plan a scene that shows Mary is anxious, think of some actions such as pacing, drumming fingers, or overreacting to an innocent comment. Assume the reader is smart enough to figure out she is anxious without telling him.

There *is* a place for narrative summary. For example, if a meeting between two characters takes place over several hours, you don't want to show every minute of this interaction and therefore must summarize the boring long pauses. Summary in small doses helps to control the pacing of your scene, and therefore is a useful tool. Balancing showing and summary takes some practice, but as you learn err on the side of showing.

Point of View (POV)

First Person: I saw. I ran. I did.
Second Person: You saw. You ran. You did.
Third Person: He saw. She ran. He did.

In grammar school you probably learned about writing in first, second, or third person. For writing a screenplay, you're only going to be able to write objective third (the camera view), so you don't have to worry about this section. However, if you are writing a novel you have important choices to make about your story's voice.

Point of View (POV) refers to the narrative structure you'll use to tell your story. In novels there are two generally used

POVs: first person, and third person. Second person has been used in a few experimental works, but it never caught on and I don't recommend this one.

Voice becomes powerful in the novel because of the ability to penetrate from the outer to the inner. While the objective voice describes only what the camera sees and hears, the penetrating or deep voice in addition to what occurs externally also describes the thoughts and feelings of one or more characters.

In the nineteenth century stories were often told in an omniscient penetrating voice: the narrator jumped at will from the head of one character to another, and described things that might not be known to anyone but the author. This style is rarely if ever used nowadays because it places too much distance between the reader and the characters. The objective voice is also seldom used today in fiction although there are a few novels with it especially in the science fiction genre.

An important rule of modern fiction for the penetrating voice is that one, and only one, character's perceptions are described during one scene. This character is called the "POV character."

In first person the POV character tells the entire story. This is the most intimate voice, and an example is John Knowles' *A Separate Peace*. Since this is a challenging voice to use, a less expert storyteller may not achieve the same effect as Knowles. The writer is limited to showing only story events known by the POV character. Occasionally the writer circumvents this problem by using more than one first person character and delineating the narrator through indicating the identity at the beginning of the section.

However, alternating between first person POV characters is awkward. Perhaps the most common voice used by modern novelists is the third person limited, with the best of both worlds: emotional and intimate descriptions, and the ability to seamlessly rotate characters.

The penetrating POV is the greatest strength of novel writing. Films of course have music, camera angles, and other tricks that make them a different, yet also strong, medium.

Here are two passages that contrast objective and penetrating POV:

Third Person Objective:
Sam ran down the hallway. It was long and there were no windows. He picked up speed. The entrance was twenty feet away.

Third Person Limited:
He had to escape.
Sam couldn't see the intruder, but knew he must be close by. This was the vulnerable section: a long white tunnel, no windows.
Twenty feet. He might just make it. If only he could turn off these lights to race in the dark, but no time, no time.
And then he heard a footstep behind him.

Did you notice the character goal stated at the beginning of the second example? This goal helps your reader to focus and know for what he should be watching as your scene unfolds. The story questions rise from this goal: Will Sam escape? Who is Sam escaping from?

Point of View is a complex topic upon which I've only touched. If this is a new concept for you, I recommend you read Orson Scott Card's *Elements of Fiction Writing: Characters and Viewpoint* for good guidance.

Tension

Tension must be in every chapter, every paragraph, and even every sentence. A good definition of tension might be: The uncertainty of at least one issue.

Tension is not generated when the writer describes exciting (or not so exciting) events that the protagonist wrestles through, but in the end these events don't push the story along. They simply add word count. For example, a POV character will find a chilled bottle of water, unscrew its tight cap, take a few sips of the cold liquid, then screw the lid back on and wipe her hands on her black summer-cloth-weight Capri pants, feeling refreshed now. If the character has arthritis then her method of opening a bottle might give a grace note to her character, but otherwise this is throwaway stuff.

So how might one push a story along? There are many techniques to do this. Perhaps the most reliable device to add tension is to include a ticking clock: a time limit to accomplish a goal.

The core principle is to consistently raise the stakes for the protagonist: put more in jeopardy, make it uncertain that the protagonist can accomplish a goal that is vital to him and for the long-term success for the story. Everything counts, including little actions. Who cares how the character opens a bottle of water? But if the character isn't sure that she will be able to sneak a sip of water to calm a cough before she has to make an announcement, it might become more interesting.

When you write a sentence, paragraph, scene, or more, ask yourself, "Do these words and events matter to the story?" If not, get rid of them.

Back Story

Back story can be defined as events that happened before the story begins. Unless handled carefully, back story will kill your reader's interest in your story by pulling him away from the forward action.

The back story is important for you the author to understand the events currently taking place in your story, but often not necessary for the reader. Before you explain the past origins of a current circumstance, ask yourself if you need to do this for the reader to enjoy the story. Be tough—more often than not you won't.

Back story is incorporated into the story as a flashback, through narrative, or through dialogue.

A flashback can be defined as a scene depicting a previous event. Since the flashback breaks the story action to insert something for which the reader has not been acclimated, it is difficult to handle well. I generally don't recommend using flashbacks.

Narrative is easier to make invisible but describing back story, even in an engaging fashion, breaks away from the forward action and thus should be done with caution if at all.

Dialogue is a notorious place to dump back story. Beware the "as you know, Bob" syndrome in which one character explains things of which the second character is already aware, for example past history of an event. A better way to handle background information is if the second character doesn't know it—then the reader can learn at the same time. For a great discussion on adding background information via dialogue, see Snyder's discussion of "Pope in the Pool" in his book *Save the Cat!*

Good writers know to make understanding the back story essential to the action of the present story. If a character must make a decision, right now, that depends on his knowledge of history, then the reader along with the character will breath-lessly anticipate learning the information.

Setting

The setting describes where your story takes place. A screen-play takes care of setting automatically, since filmed scenes (or those performed on stage) take place within a physical context. However, when writing a novel only words stand between you and the reader. You need to imbue a sense of place without over-whelming the reader.

Describing a room or a person in excruciating physical detail exhausts the reader as he tries to build a visual picture. A few specific and unusual details are much better. For example, if you're trying to convey a sense of refinement describe the roaring fire in the hand-worked marble fireplace, the burnished wood of the antiques, and the Waterford crystal glasses near the wet bar in the corner.

Alternatively, including too few details makes the story occur in a vacuum for the reader. If you forget to describe the physical context of a scene in the heat of writing, remember to go back to add the details. Setting can be described in one dedi-cated paragraph, then details added as necessary throughout the remainder of the scene. Sue Grafton makes good use of this technique.

A good trick to elevate the setting from background to playing a role in the story is to describe the POV character's internal reactions to the person or place, or implicitly through descrip-tive words he might use. For example, one character might see the darkening sky ahead as threatening whereas another might see it as invigorating. What the character notices is also suggestive. Does he see the rack of guns in the corner or the daisies in a vase on the table?

Finally, if you're building an alternate world remember to put limits on any magical powers or circumstances you invent. These limits make the story world seem "real." Even Superman is vulnerable to Kryptonite.

Research

Here's the short and easy take home message: Don't fake your facts. Someone, somewhere, is going to find you out. Call universities, museums, science labs, accounting offices, veterinary hospitals, or other places having people who know what you need to know. Be polite and keep calling until you're connected with one or more experts. Tell the person you are a writer. Most of the time the expert is delighted to talk with you provided the conversation is no more than about ten minutes. Explain what you want to do in your story, then ask the expert if this is a reasonable scenario. Let the expert discuss and suggest things—you stay quiet and take notes.

When you've written your section(s) ask the expert if he would read what you wrote to make sure it makes sense. Finally, acknowledge the expert's help in your published book or manu-script.

Dialogue

If a writer wrote "real" dialogue it would be boring:

Jen: *"Hi Roger. How's it been?"*
Roger: *"I'm doing okay, I guess."*
Jen: *"Um, I was just leaving. I'm still working on that report."*

Roger: *"Oh man, I hate doing those. Smith gave me, ah, three last week."*

Jen: *"That's tough. Uh... Well, see you around."*

You get the point that every line of dialogue must have a purpose. Dialogue has a verisimilitude (appearance of reality) but it is not what people actually say to each other: dialogue is concise, and flows to topics rather than stays in one place. Screenplays are composed of dialogue. In novels the open appearance of dialogue on the page gives a nice break for the reader. Make the words count.

Dialogue needs a purpose and builds to something. Here's an example of a character question and some possible tangents:

Emily: *"Do you like eggs for breakfast?"*

Tim: (answer one) *"Yes."*

Tim: (answer two) *"My mom used to make eggs, soft boiled, you know, and she'd break them over toast so that the egg yolk would soak in."*

Tim: (answer three) *"Why is it any of your business?"*

Answer one stops the conversation, and the story. There are times when this answer might be appropriate, but in general, answers two or three might be a better choice. Answer two opens a chance to deepen character background in a natural way, and answer three suggests a brewing fight. My general rule for questions in writing, whether in dialogue or the story events, is never to put down a direct answer unless you are pulling off a specific, deliberate effect.

You need to make it easy to follow who is saying what. Often a speech tag can be replaced by a beat (a small action). *He started.*

"Are you kidding?" When using a speech tag, stick to "said" and "asked" since these are invisible. Other tags (gasped, shuddered, mouthed, and so forth) call attention to themselves, something you don't want to do.

Have your characters say unexpected things, and be concise in your wording.

Watch profanity. An occasional slipped cuss might be okay for emphasis, but look upon it as a challenge to get around using profanity even if your character is the type who regularly would. Can you demonstrate a character's disgust through his actions, say spitting, rather than an f-bomb? Perhaps you can summarize: *"He cursed."* If you must have an expletive, consider if using a benign word like *"Blast!"* might work.

Occasionally you will have a foreign character for whom you wish to convey his differently-sounding speech. A good way *not* to do this is using strange spelling and apostrophes. For example, reading *"Git ovah heah! I 'as ta speak ta ya"* takes the reader a moment to translate what the speaker is saying. Reading much more than this isolated line becomes fatiguing.

Instead of alternate word spellings, to delineate a foreign speaker good writers will employ an occasional transposed word or develop a unique phrase or exclamation to identify the particular speaker. No difficult spellings or translations are needed. One might write, *"Yikees. Is good for this to be put down over his head, and to rest there let it be."*

Motivation Reaction Units (MRUs)

Dwight Swain first described these. MRUs are the smallest units by which a story is told, and when these are consistently used correctly your story will powerfully draw in the reader.

There are two parts of the MRU, the stimulus (cause) and the response (effect), that string together to form a narrative.

The stimulus is external to your character. In other words, it is something occurring in the environment that could be seen, heard and/or touched by any character in that location. It should be significant to your POV character so that he will feel he needs to respond. Some examples of a stimulus might be a dog breaking its leash and viciously growling as it runs toward the POV character, the hard-won note with secret information fluttering from the POV character's pocket, or the POV character's love interest whom he thought hated him unexpectedly kissing him.

The POV character is not written as the subject of the stimulus because this distances the reader from your character. In other words, you would say, *"The drawer pinched Sharon's finger,"* not *"Sharon felt the drawer pinch her finger."*

The response describes your character's reaction to the stimulus, and must occur after the stimulus. In other words, you wouldn't say, *"Sharon yelped and pulled her hand away after the drawer pinched her finger"* because this is out of order. First Sharon feels the pinch, then she reacts. This may sound obvious, but it happens more frequently than you might expect. Although the reader may not identify the reversed order, he will feel as if something is off.

The response has four components that must always be in the correct order. These components are: emotion or sensation, reflex action, rational action, and speech. For example:

A loud crack ripped through the canyon. (stimulus)
Jack started (emotion/sensation) *then looked up in the direction of the sound.* (reflex action) *The careening boulder was*

almost on him and he grabbed the bush to pull himself out of the way. (rational action) *"Too close," he said.* (speech)

The boulder thumped where he had stood a moment before. (stimulus*) He felt the ground vibrate* (emotion/sensation) *and shivered.* (reflex action) *He hadn't escaped yet.* (rational action)

"Ryan, we've got to get out of here now!"(speech)

Most of the time you will not use all four of these response components. When you use fewer than four, just make sure that the ones you do use are in the correct order.

When should you use all of these reaction components at once? Since these components intensify the reader experience, you use all four when you want to increase tension or else to highlight something important.

Put Your Best Writing Up Front

Always put your best writing up front. Don't hold anything in reserve.

The writer often feels (even if not articulated) that he or she isn't capable of writing at this high level of quality throughout the whole manuscript. And in a sense this may be true, but there is a wonderful technique called cutting and pasting that's so easy. Simply go through your manuscript and cut the bad stuff, put all the good stuff end to end, then fill in the holes.

The bigger hurdle for the writer often is the sense of inadequacy: you may feel you were lucky with this one scene, but couldn't do it again.

Yes you can. Have faith in yourself. If you use up all of your good stuff, you're going to have to come up with more that is just as good. And you will. Many studies have shown that the best way to become skilled in an area is, surprise, doing it. So keep writing, even if it stinks, and when something's good copy and paste it in your end-to-end file. You'll be amazed at how this file begins to grow into a gripping story.

LEVEL SEVEN:

Refining

You are now on the seventh level of story construction. On this level you're going to polish your first draft. Did you ever think you'd make it this far? Congratulations! You'll also learn how writers typically proceed after they have a finished manuscript. When you're finished this level you may be ready to find an agent, publisher, or producer for your work.

Chapter Sixteen

Editing and Criticism

Writing a book or screenplay is a solitary enterprise, but you don't have to remain completely alone. It can be affirming to find a few others, or even one other writer, who understands this strange occupation of building worlds in your head. You may want to think about attending a writing conference, and/or joining a writing or critique group of fellow writers.

Writing Conferences

Writing conferences can be encouraging places to meet other writers as well as editors, producers, and agents. They can be wonderfully renewing experiences for writers of many skill levels, ranging from thinking-about-it to multi-published.

Conferences vary in size and quality, so you'll want to investigate before putting money down to register. Do you want to focus on a specialty area or something more general? How far away can you travel, and for how long can you stay? Check out who are the speakers and faculty, and make sure there are at least a few you'd like to meet.

Conferences are typically comprised of lectures as well as one or more brief individual appointments with the professionals. Normally for the appointment you'll pitch your story to the agent or editor, and hope that you might be able to spark some interest. Be prepared: before the conference put together a proposal, a synopsis, and the first few sparkling pages of your manuscript just in case the person asks to see something. You also need to rehearse your logline and elevator speech (thirty second summary) so when the person says, "Tell me about your story," you'll be able to coherently answer.

Chances are that you'll also informally meet agents and editors at meal times and other times throughout the conference. It's difficult, but remember not to be a pest or to be over-eager to push your work on them. You'll have a position of power if you can step back and be relaxed about meeting people. Chat and ask how they liked their trip. Find out a little about them instead of talking *at* them incessantly. It is often a tiring experience for the agent or editor to be on display for the few days of the conference, so be kind.

Don't forget to bring your business cards to pass out as you meet your fellow writers.

Writing Groups

Groups vary in approach and what they do. Some are mostly supportive, while others take critiquing or other activities to a serious level. It may take some time to find what you like, but keep at it.

Online groups offer a wide variety of subspecialties of writing. These tend toward trading critiques of members' manuscripts. You can search under yahoo groups or other internet groups, or form your own.

To find a group that meets in your area, check with libraries, bookstores, churches, schools, and other places where writers might be expected to congregate. And as always, check the internet for possible leads.

Giving Criticism

The best critiques balance suggesting changes with noting good qualities. Even if you're critiquing the most abysmal thing imaginable, remember there is a person behind the words you're marking up, and be kind. That person has shown courage to let someone else (you) see her "baby." In my own experience nonfiction does not have nearly the sense of personal exposure that fiction does.

I like to couch my feedback in "I" statements—"I was confused by this passage," "I didn't think this was a realistic development in the story," and so forth. This technique softens the author's sense of being attacked because you're describing your impression, not an absolute fact. You do no favors if you don't point out possible problems you're noticing. Be gentle, but be honest.

The person who has asked for your opinion is likely sensitive and highly concerned with even the smallest clues regarding like and dislike. If the person you are critiquing is a new writer, too-harsh comments may even squash the fragile desire to learn to write. Please remember this and be careful. You wield power with your words.

Receiving Criticism

Two of my favorite phrases I like to remember when receiving criticism are from the book of Proverbs: "As iron sharpens iron, so one man sharpens another," (Proverbs 27:17) and "Faithful are the wounds of a friend; profuse are the kisses of an enemy." (Proverbs 27:6)

As writers, we have all experienced negative responses to our work. Sometimes criticism is given in the best spirit, to help and to improve. Sometimes it is motivated out of jealousy or generalized misanthropy. Sometimes the critiquer is simply not qualified to give a helpful opinion.

It doesn't matter. The best way to respond to criticism is to say, "Thank you." Period. Don't defend yourself since you won't change someone's opinion. Take the words back with you and study them. Maintain an objective stance (it may take a little time to get there). If the words are pointing out something true, then internalize the message and learn from it. If the words aren't relevant, discard them. This may be difficult, of course, but is the best way to go.

When someone flags a passage of your manuscript, he often does not correctly identify the problem. For example, the person may call it a character issue, but the problem may simply be truncating an emotional scene. It is your job to figure this out. When more than one person points to the same passage, scrutinize it with a microscope. Comments are the best way to improve and grow. Even the mean comments can be helpful.

Self-Editing

Writing and editing are two different functions, and it's difficult to switch between them. It takes less emotional energy to edit, so I recommend that you concentrate on finishing your first draft before starting a major effort to fix the words. However, this section gives notice that you aren't finished when you type "The End" at the bottom of your manuscript. There's still much work to do before you'll be ready to search for an agent or editor, or to publish this yourself. I have more information in Chapter Seventeen and Appendix Five.

The bar for publishing is high, and your manuscript must sparkle before you send it out. You have only one chance to get this right.

Good ways are available for getting feedback and editing for your manuscript. One way is to join a critique group as above, either online or locally. Books about self-editing are available; I've listed a few good ones in Appendix One. And of course some people hire editors to go over their work.

While "editing" can fall into different categories such as grammar, punctuation, wording, idea structuring, and so forth, for this book I want to focus on the common problem of manuscript length. Please note that you shouldn't worry about length until you've finished your first draft. However, once you have finished and are thinking about submitting your work to agents or editors, or self-publishing it, length is something to pay attention to.

The word count of a newly finished manuscript is often beyond the outer acceptable publishing guidelines. These guidelines vary depending on genre and publishing house, but rule of thumb lengths might be 50,000 words for a short novel, 80-90,000 words for a standard size, and nothing from a newbie longer than 100,000 words.

The publishing guidelines for length are important. Readers in different genres expect a particular length, especially from an unknown author. Furthermore, publishing books is a business with a slim profit margin, and paper books are expensive to produce. Even with the growing popularity of e-books, at this time paper books remain a critical venue to make sales. For example, it's easier to sell a paper book than e-book in a store or at a book signing, and it's more elegant to give a paper book than e-book as a gift. If you are a newbie writer with a too-long manuscript you must justify increased retail price and/or a smaller margin of profit to print a paper book. With so many manuscripts available the publisher can more easily start with a different one than yours.

However, in my opinion too-high word count is most worrisome to a publisher because it suggests too much verbiage. Here is my rule of thumb for unpublished writers: Once you think your manuscript is absolutely, positively ready, you should be able to cut at least ten percent.

How can you do this fine cutting?

It's easier to do several passes and concentrate on one kind of systematic error at a time. There is no point at which you are "finished," so the more times you go through your manuscript, the tighter and better you will make it.

How you edit will depend on what works for you. Here's a possible method you can use:

First Pass

Transfer all of the reader feedback that you agree with.

Second Pass

From reader comments and your own observations, determine your particular writing tics—words or phrases that you overuse. You may want to check out http://www.wordcounter.com/ or a similar website that counts the incidence of words in a sample of text.

Third Pass

Use the computer word search function to eliminate "very," "quite," "began to," "started to," "somewhat," "rather," and other nothing qualifiers. Remove words that end in -ly and other modifiers and adverbs/adverbial phrases, and replace the core verbs and nouns with stronger ones. An occasional modifier is fine, but verify that you don't do Noah's Ark where the modifiers come two by two. (*The sleek and dark cat was looking for a quick, tasty dinner as it ran toward the tiny, bulging mouse.*). For Noah's Ark, use the single strongest word/description or else delete modifiers entirely. (*The cat was looking for dinner as it ran toward the bulging mouse.*).

Fourth Pass

Use the word search for said, asked, and other speech tags. Eliminate as many of these as you can. If you need clarity in the conversations, instead of a speech tag try using an occasional beat or small action. *"What do you mean?" She pounded the table.* Only use a speech tag for clarity if you must.

Fifth Pass

To eliminate passive voice, use the computer grammar checker and/or the word search function to find "was," "were," "have," and similar words. Rewrite these sentences in active construction.

Sixth Pass

Read carefully through your manuscript. Every time you describe something, or have a character speak, ask yourself "Is this necessary to the story?" Don't keep anything extraneous.

The following exercises give a reasonable series of actions for editing your manuscript. These later tuning steps should be done several times. Once you've edited your manuscript, give it to another reader to incorporate his suggestions and comments.

Be cautious: The more times you or another reader read your manuscript, the "colder" you or he will become to it. Read word-for-word as little as you can—use the computer search function to bring you to correctable places, then move on. After each read-through, let your mind rest from it as long as possible before starting again.

Exercise 104: Mapping Your Story

List every scene of your story if you haven't already done so. Determine the author purpose of each scene and consider: Can you remove it or combine it with another scene?

Exercise 105: Word Searches

Use your word search function to eliminate word tics and nothing words such as "very," "quite," "began to," "started to," "rather," and so forth. Eliminate adverbs (words ending in –ly). Find speech tags (said, asked, etc.) and eliminate them if possible.

Exercise 106: Passive Voice

Use your grammar checker and word search functions to find passages with passive voice. Reword these.

Exercise 107: The Rest of the Story

You may wish to work with your manuscript in blocks of about twenty-five double-spaced pages at a time to decrease fatigue. Start reading from the beginning. Evaluate each section, paragraph, sentence, and word to decide if it's necessary or if it could be better written. Consider also from the reader's perspective the order of the information. Are description, action, and motivation clear? Does anything need to be rearranged?

Conclusion

A friend uses a trick to reduce her manuscript word count: she removes one word from each sentence, or even one word from each paragraph. These deletes add up.

This final editing process will amaze you as you see how much stronger your story becomes. See Appendix Four for a sample edit.

Chapter Seventeen

Submitting a Manuscript

You've finished and edited your manuscript and now are thinking about publishing or producing your story. Congratulations! By writing something front to back, you've accomplished a goal that most people dream of but never do. Enjoy the moment.

A Word of Warning

You have many choices and nuts-and-bolts steps you can take to gain access to traditional publishing or a production company, or to produce a self-published book. However, the most important thing no one seems to talk about, is before you start investing time to find a literary or film agent, or put money down to publish/produce yourself, you must honestly ask:

IS MY NOVEL OR SCREENPLAY
READY TO GO AHEAD?

My experience with most of the newbie manuscripts I've seen is that significant problems exist that likely will disqualify the manuscript from successfully competing in the field. For example, the author might need to cut about a fifth of the manuscript, put in better transitions, or write a satisfying ending.

Hold out the standard that your book or screenplay will be as good as anything else out there—because it must be.

Screenwriting Submissions

The submission package for a screenplay is similar but not identical to that of a novel. You should polish your logline to a high sheen, and prepare a one page query letter and a 250 word (one page) synopsis. This synopsis is different from the pitch you wrote in Chapter Ten, since it briefly summarizes your story rather than acts as a teaser. (You can use your pitch in your query letter). For this synopsis include your critical scenes, a brief description of important characters as they appear, and your story's conclusion. Write it in third person present tense.

You'll also need to prepare a film treatment, although the agent doesn't always request this. The treatment covers each scene in your story, compressed into about twenty-five pages. Again, third person present tense.

You may wish to prepare a character list giving a brief description of each person in your story.

Finally, you need to polish your screenplay. The specific requirements of a screenplay are beyond the scope of this book, but check Appendix One for some good resources. The screenplay should be about 120 pages.

When you write to the agent, include your contact information, SASE (self-addressed stamped envelope) for a letter, and another stamped envelope for return of your materials.

Types of Book Publishing: Traditional or Self?

If you've written a novel, you need to determine what sort of author you want to be:

— Someone who anticipates selling a personal story to a small group of people.
— Someone who wishes to sell books commercially on the internet and other venues.
— Someone who wants to be a blockbuster author with a twenty city tour, an appearance on Oprah, and a movie deal. Well, we all can dream, can't we?

Very Small Time Publishing

If you have only a limited and well-defined group for sales, say a club, church, or family, you'll have to take the initiative to publish your manuscript because a traditional press such as Random House won't be interested. Unless you are a desktop publisher (not an unreasonable solution), your best option may be to go to a subsidy press that will walk you through the publishing maze, give you a certain number of books, and maybe even get your book available on the internet so your friends can purchase it easily.

I advise you investigate several companies before you sign with one, since the quality of services and economic value varies from excellent to steal-you-blind. Mark Levine compares a number of companies and ranks them in his book *The Fine Print of Self-Publishing*. Read this book to understand how subsidy companies function and for what you need to look out.

Commercial Sales

If you want to sell books commercially, you need to be more careful about how you publish. This is not an easy decision since there are significant positives and negatives to each option. Broadly, your choices are:

1. Traditional Publishing
2. Subsidy Publishing
3. Self-Publishing
4. E-Publishing

Let's look at some advantages and disadvantages of each of these.

Traditional Publishing

Traditional publishing is a difficult field to break into, but if you can make it, it offers strong advantages. Your manuscript will be read and edited multiple times by different viewers, and therefore your published book will be polished and well written. You will have a beautiful cover. Rather than paying to produce the book, you will receive money: an advance upon signing the contract, and regular royalty checks once you have "earned back" your advance through book sales. Perhaps most importantly, you'll have a marketing machine behind you so will bypass many hurdles that self-published books have to jump. Your book will be available in brick and mortar (physical) stores, and you may even be able to obtain a book tour or other publicity opportunities from your publisher.

The biggest drawback to traditional publishing is that you no longer own your book. If the publisher wants to change text, or discontinue the run, or do anything else, you can't prevent it.

Subsidy and Print on Demand Publishing

Subsidy or print on demand publishing occurs when you pay a company to produce a paper book for you under their imprint. This is not self-publishing because it is the company publishing you, although using a subsidy press is often called self-publishing.

Beyond the book's being listed with online bookstores such as Amazon and Barnes & Noble, there usually is little or no help with marketing. (This is also true with self-publishing). The author will probably give up rights to some aspects of the book such as ISBN and physical files of cover and typesetting. He may also give up other rights depending on the contract.

Subsidy companies vary in quality and cost, and there are definitely some good ones; depending on goals, many people are satisfied publishing this way. If you decide to go this route I recommend you first read *The Fine Print of Self-Publishing* and research several companies before signing any contract. Some advantages with using subsidy publishing are that final books can often be produced within a matter of weeks, and they are usually attractive.

See Appendix Five for more information.

Self Publishing

A self-publisher forms his own company to print a paper book. The major advantage of self-publishing is complete control to produce an excellent product and keep all rights to it. The downside is the need to coordinate all details. Producing a book can be expensive, although it doesn't have to be. Furthermore, the self-publisher depends solely on his own platform and marketing resources to sell the book (This is almost certainly true of subsidy publishing as well).

Many resources are available to develop your own self-publishing company. See Appendix One and Appendix Five for a start.

E-Publishing

Online giant bookseller Amazon reported in the summer of 2010 that Kindle e-books outsold hardcover books, and a few months later in 2011 that Kindle e-books outsold all print books. The penetration of the e-reader into the publishing market will only continue.

If you own your book's rights you can easily prepare, format, and e-publish your manuscript for no cost using conversion software on Amazon and Barnes & Noble, or hire someone to design a cover and/or optimally format your book for a little money. You own the book's rights if this will be the only place you publish, you have formed your own company to self-publish, or you have not signed these rights away with a subsidy company. For the latter, some companies take these rights, some don't.

Broadly speaking, there are three formats of e-book: mobi, which is read on the Amazon Kindle; ePub, which is the default for most other e-readers including the Barnes & Noble Nook; and PDF files which can be read on computers and e-readers.

See Appendix Five for more information about e-publishing.

Traditional Publishing

"Traditional Publishing" is what most people think of for producing a book. These are the companies such as Harper Collins, Thomas Nelson, or Random House. Entering the gates as a newbie writer is not an easy task, but if you can do it this method offers significant advantages.

The two most common ways to make contact with a publishing house are through an editor at the house, or through a literary agent. Normally the writer sends a query letter and possibly submission materials to said editor or agent. These can be sent cold or after an invitation, say at a writer's conference. Going for an agent rather than an editor is highly recommended, according to Noah Lukeman who is a literary agent and has written several books about this process (see Appendix One). He affirms that the writer may need to query fifty or more literary agents before he is able to find representation.

Once you have found a literary agent, the agent uses his knowledge of different editors, houses, and the publishing business to shop your manuscript; he hopes to get an acquiring editor to say yes. When an editor agrees, he (the editor) shepherds the manuscript through several committees at the publishing house as they determine whether, on balance, this is a good manuscript to acquire.

When your manuscript is accepted by the publishing house, the agent negotiates an advantageous deal for you. This includes aspects such as advance money, the ability to have a say in cover design, the number of influencer copies of books you'll receive, possible tours and other resources for marketing, and whatever else might be important. Your release date will usually be a year to eighteen months from the time your manuscript is accepted. You'll be paid an advance against royalties: this is money that the publishing company thinks the book will make. You don't have to pay this money back even if the book doesn't make the expected profit. The manuscript goes through several edits, a cover is designed, back cover copy is written, facts are checked, and on and on to make your book as perfect as possible. The publicity department is called in to determine a good strategy for selling the book.

Next, your book needs endorsements. The house prints Advance Reader Copies (ARCs), which are books without final corrections and therefore containing slight errors. You, the acquiring editor, others in the publishing house, and your agent determine who would be likely people or book review sites from whom to receive endorsements.

Finally, your book's release date arrives. Your book is now available for sale in brick and mortar (physical) stores and through online stores such as Amazon and Barnes & Noble. You work to publicize your book (book tours, interviews, book signings, etc.), and hopefully sell a million copies. You'll be paid a percent of the book price for each book sold after you have earned enough in sales to cover the advance money. This may not happen, and if so indicates that yours was a losing book for the publishing house to acquire. Your sales figures will be evaluated carefully when you're ready to publish your next manuscript.

A Sparkling Submission Package

Writers often spend months or even years writing a novel, and next to no time preparing submission materials to find a home for it. This is a big mistake—a poorly compiled presentation will doom your manuscript to failure even if you've written the next *Gone with the Wind*. Take some time to craft an exceptional submission package.

Items you should prepare before beginning the submission process include a one-page query letter, short and long synopsis, and a book proposal including a marketing plan (see Appendix One for books about writing proposals). You should also highly polish at least the first twenty-five pages (or three chapters) of your manuscript.

Exercise 108: Book Positioning

You need to understand how to position and present your story. What is your manuscript's genre? Some examples are romance, adventure, mystery, suspense, etc. What are some similar books? What are some unusual characteristics of your story?

Exercise 109: Book Length

How long is your manuscript? Is this length appropriate for your genre? Many publishers, especially of romances, give strict word limits, and all genres have "typical" word ranges. A manuscript over 100,000 words will be a serious strike against you no matter what the genre; try to pare it down to 80-90,000 words at the most. See Chapter Sixteen for editing tips.

Exercise 110: Logline and Pitch

Review and rewrite your logline (Exercise 22) and pitch (Exercise 63) for the submission package.

The One-Page Query Letter

You send a one-page query letter to the editor(s) or preferably the agent(s) of interest. Sometimes the person also wants to receive a short synopsis and/or a few pages of the manuscript. Do your research and send what is requested, no more, no less. When in doubt send just a query.

Remember to make it easy for the agent/editor to respond to you if they want more. Include your e-mail, snail mail, and telephone numbers. If you're mailing by snail mail, include a SASE (self-addressed stamped envelope) for a response letter. If you e-mail your query, make sure that hitting reply won't cause the e-mail to bounce or cause the agent/editor to prove that he is a real person in order for the e-mail to reach you. If you query by e-mail you should query directly in the text, not attach the letter as a separate document since many agents and editors worry about computer viruses. Please don't call the agent or editor to pitch a story. He won't appreciate being interrupted.

You may send out fifty or more queries before you get a nibble, so put on your emotional armor before you start the process. This is the way the publishing business works.

The purpose of the query letter is to hook the interest of your prospect. It's tempting to put in a lot of information, but you should instead make your query short and intriguing. Use your logline and pitch.

According to Noah Lukeman in *Writing the Query Letter*, the query has four general parts:

1. Introduction. Why are you writing to this particular person? Target your reason.
2. Intrigue. Tell a little about the story, enough to raise curiosity without killing it.
3. Justify. What is your background that makes you qualified to write and sell this story?
4. Close. State specifically the action the person can take if he is interested.

And to contradict what was said above, here is a sample query from the Preditors and Editors web site:

Dear Mr. Agent:

What if the President of the United States committed a murder in front of you? What if you were a member of his Secret Service protection? Would you arrest him? Would you report the crime? Or would you cover up the crime to protect the nation because of an international crisis?

These are the questions Shari Nichols must resolve in my novel, ALL FALL DOWN. At the moment of the murder she professes allegiance to President Halverson, but she questions whether she has made the right choice. A quick promotion puts her into a job that consumes her attention and seems to support the President's action of murder. But within weeks a series of events makes Shari wonder if the President is as honorable as he seems. Shari Nichols digs for the truth and unearths secrets woven deeply within the infrastructure of the government. Secrets that touch even her family, but she may be digging her own grave.

The completed manuscript is available upon request. A SASE is included for your convenience. Thank you for your generous time. I look forward to hearing from you soon.

Cordially,

Submitting your work for publication is a tedious process that requires much patience, research, and a thick skin.

Publication and Marketing

Many people seem to think that once they hold the book in their hands, the journey and the work is over. While this is an amazing moment, it is just the beginning. If you want anyone to purchase your book, you must market.

Here are some marketing ideas:

Book Review Sites

The period of weeks before your publication date is valuable time that you won't recapture to promote your title. Traditional publishers send out books for review and endorsements about three to six months before release. If you self-publish, you will need to look into this yourself.

Endorsers

Endorsements are important to get. If you are traditionally published, your publisher (and agent if you have one) will help with these. Especially if you're self-published, make a list of your dream endorsers: authors who have written similar books and experts in your book's field. Then, think of more accessible potential endorsers: authors in your critique group, professors at the local college, and friends especially with educational degrees or other credentials. A writer's conference or a writer's loop are more good places to ask for endorsements.

Influencers

Influencers are so named because they can influence others if they like your book. Some things an influencer can do is tell her friends and book clubs about your book, ask her local library to order it, and write an online site review for Amazon or Barnes & Noble.

Influencers are a wonderful, humble way to get the word out. Not only do you get valuable feedback and facilitate further sales, but many authors enjoy meeting or e-meeting so many people. The influencers are also excited to meet a real, live author.

Online Reviews

Online book reviews at sites like Amazon and Barnes and Noble are valuable because they're objective. When you pursue reviews, remember that the reviewer may not necessarily give a five-star "great book!" endorsement, so make sure your book really is good and consider your strategies accordingly.

United States Federal Trade Commission rules now mandate that free books given for review must have this fact stated in the review.

Website

Your website is the reader's major source of information and point of contact for you and your book. You must have one.

Platform

The author's platform describes the people he comes into contact with and with whom he can talk about his book through the internet (Twitter, Facebook, blogging), biography line for written articles, and direct contact (speaking engagements, classes, and so forth). Think of ways to get your name and book in front of people.

Blog Tours

The internet creates opportunities to network and disseminate information. A twist on the old-fashioned book tour is the Blog Tour, where a single book is featured within a short period of time on multiple blogs. Since the blog reviewers give honest opinions of the bad as well as the good, a potential buyer can make a reasonable assessment of whether he might actually like the book.

Postcards

Postcards are a great marketing tool, and you can receive them relatively cheaply from an online printing company. One side of the card should have the front cover image of your book. The other side should include book information such as your back cover copy, your best endorsement or two, and maybe your biography. Include your underlined website(s), ISBN, and contact/order info.

Book Clubs

Oprah has made them famous. Ask at the library, nearby bookstores, colleges, and your church or synagogue for book clubs that meet in your area. Call up the leaders and ask if they'd like to have you, the author, present to the group or help facilitate a meeting. Make a list of discussion questions.

Book Signings at Bookstores or Other Places

Post flyers so people know about the event. Think of how you will autograph your books, for example including a short phrase before your signature. When you show up the day of the signing, bring chocolates or cookies and plenty of books.

Tangential Interest Areas of the Book

Bookstores are not the only places where books are sold. If your book is about, say, a teenage anorectic skater then you might be able to have the local ice skating rink sponsor a book signing and/or carry the books. You also may be able to arrange a speaking engagement for teens on anorexia (or how to write a book) at a local church or library.

This is not a final list, of course; any legal/moral/ethical method you find to sell books is good. Be creative! See Appendix One for a few resources that can get you started with marketing.

Chapter Eighteen

Conclusion

So that's it, everything I know about structuring a story plus a few more tidbits.

Congratulations for making it to this point, because this means you are taking your writing goal seriously and trusting that you can create a good novel or screenplay. You can. You may be like the gentleman I work with now who strengthened his resolve in a difficult job by telling himself he'd write a novel when he was retired. Well, he's retired now, but was almost ready to throw away a thirty year old dream until he stopped writing "organically" and started employing some of the principles here. This is my deep hope for this book: that it helps you to fulfill your driving dream. You can do it!

God bless you, and happy writing.

List of Exercises

Index

C

D

E

F

G

H

I

Q

R

S

Glossary

Acclimation Beat– a common beat occurring in act two/part one, right after the switch away beat. The acclimation beat is low key and shows the protagonist looking around the new world for the first time.

Act One – first quarter of the story. This section is comprised of ordinary world, inciting incident, argument, and door.

Act Two/Part One – second quarter of the story. This section may include switch away beat and acclimation beat. This section is comprised of three or four increasingly intense conflicts. It ends with the midpoint.

Act Two/Part Two – third quarter of the story. This section is often comprised of hidden need triplet, protagonist disintegrates, antagonists get stronger, and ends with the slide.

Act Three – last quarter of the story. This section is comprised of preparation for battle with crazy plan, then a series of battles between protagonist and antagonist ending with the stereotyped sequence of darkest moment, help from outside, climax, and resolution.

Advance against Royalties – monies that are paid by the publisher to the author before book is produced.

Advance Reader Copy (ARC) – preliminary book without final corrections that is printed close to book release date and used to receive endorsements.

Antagonist –adversary to the protagonist.

Antagonists Get Stronger – stage in act two/part two in which antagonists succeed in their plans. Originally identified by Blake Snyder in *Save the Cat!*

ARC – see advance reader copy.

Argument – stage in act one in which the protagonist prepares to accept the inciting incident's invitation into the new world of act two.

Background character – walk-on characters that don't affect the story (waitress, taxi driver etc.).

Back Story – events that happened before the story begins.

Battle –external story device in which protagonist wrestles with obstacles or antagonist.

Beat – a small action.

Brick and Mortar Store – a physical book store.

Bridging Story Goal – impels the protagonist forward to take action in act one.

Bubble – a unit of story construction that bridges the gap between the "high concept" ideas for the story and individual scenes. Sometimes known as a "beat" in screenwriting (although not in this book).

Character Arc – emotional change in a character between the beginning and end of the story.

Character Goal – what the character wants.

Character Role – roles expanded upon by Pearson. The protagonist fulfills a different role in each story quarter:
orphan (act one), wanderer (act two/part one), warrior (act two/part two), martyr (act three).

Character Template – stages of character emotional change from identity to core.

The stages are: set-up, glimpse, straddling, fear, living the core, journey is completed (destiny).

CIP Data – cataloguing in publication data; categorization of book subject so that it can be easily organized by a librarian into the library system.

Climax – final, usually spectacular, battle between protagonist and antagonist in which the protagonist wins.

Confidante – character who listens to protagonist's impressions of story events and offers advice and encouragement.

Core – truest emotional description of character.

Crazy Plan – developed by protagonist in act three that is unlikely, but if everything goes correctly it may be able to defeat antagonist.

Critique Group – a group of fellow writers giving and receiving feedback on their writing.

Darkest Moment – lowest moment in act three in which the protagonist is about to die, and antagonist is about to win the story question.

Door – last event of act one in which the protagonist takes a journey of some sort into the new world of act two.

Elevator Speech – compelling spoken summary of story that can be recited in thirty seconds.

E-Pub file – a type of e-book file that can be read on Nook, Sony reader, and most other e-readers except for Amazon Kindle.

E-Publishing – a type of publishing in which books are translated into an electronic file that can be read on a computer or e-reader.

E-Reader – electronic gadget that allows reading of E-books.

Endorsement – quote from an expert or other person recommending the book.

External Obstacle – external problem that holds the protagonist back from achieving his goal. Some examples are a person who fights the protagonist or a physical barrier that must be crossed in order to move ahead.

External Story—could be seen by a camera; the physical actions that make up the story.

Fillip – a final event or piece of information after the climax that ties an unexpected end or casts the story events into a new light. A common fillip is the clichéd hint that the antagonist may rise again to threaten the protagonist or others.

Five W's and H – why, who, when, where, what, how. These are used to preplan a scene.

Flashback – scene of a previous story event.

Free-writing – talking to yourself on paper to solve problems.

Genre – Standard story classification. Some examples of genre are adventure, mystery, romance, etc.

Gift at Climax – a type of subplot that delivers a critical tool or rescue to the protagonist at the story climax. Story Strand D.

Help from Outside – right after the darkest moment in act three, a small action from someone or something outside the protagonist that allows the protagonist to regroup and win. This help does not cause the protagonist to win, but offers an opportunity and hope.

Hidden Need – an emotional lack in the protagonist that hurts others, and is solved during the course of the story. (Story Strand B).

Hidden Need Triplet – usually present in act two/part two, solves the protagonist's hidden need in a three part sequence: the hidden need is shown, the hidden need is solved, and the hidden need is demonstrated to be solved.

Hook – a compelling first line to a story that draws in the reader.

How Bad is the Antagonist – a common beat occurring in act two/part two that demonstrates (often to a protagonist's mirror) the very worst of which the antagonist is capable or a terrifying vision of what might happen if the protagonist fails in his quest.

Identity – protagonist's outer personality that he maintains to emotionally protect himself.

Inciting Incident – occurs in act one, and offers a potential change from protagonist's ordinary world, either a choice or an assignment.

Influencer – someone who agrees to promote an author's book, for example by blogging about it or hosting a book signing.

Internal Obstacle – Internal problem that holds the protagonist back from achieving his goal. Some examples are doubt, anger, and confusion.

Internal Story – thoughts and emotions of the POV characters.

ISBN – International Standard Book Number; unique identifying number for a book.

Journey – another name for the door in act one, in which the protagonist moves from old world to new world.

LCCN – Library of Congress Control Number; a unique identification number for a book in the Library of Congress' catalog record.

Literary Agent – a person who acts for the author and as an intermediary to publishing houses. A good literary agent matches manuscripts with the editors who are most likely to want them.

LLC – Limited Liability Corporation; a legal hybrid between a sole proprietorship and incorporation.

Logline – one sentence of about 15-20 words that summarizes the story.

Martyr – The protagonist role in act three. Pearson expands on this topic.

Midpoint – last event of act two/part one, an often spectacular event that is either a false high or disaster. Once the midpoint occurs, the protagonist cannot return to his old world unchanged.

Midpoint False High – midpoint type in which the protagonist seemingly conquers the new world using old way of thinking. Followed by appearance of primary antagonist in act two/part two. Occurs when primary antagonist is not known before midpoint.

Midpoint Disaster – midpoint type in which the protagonist suffers a devastating loss. Occurs when primary antagonist is known before midpoint.

Minimal Stages of a Story – described by John Truby in *The Anatomy of Story*. Stages are: weakness/need, desire, opponent, plan, battle, self-revelation, and new equilibrium.

Mobi File – a type of e-book file that can be read on Amazon Kindle and IPad.

Motivation-Reaction Unit (MRU) – smallest unit by which a story is told. Made up of stimulus (cause) and response (effect) that string together to form a narrative.

MRU – see motivation reaction unit.

New World – appears after the Door, a new place or "world" or set of circumstances offered by the inciting incident, in which the protagonist must learn to navigate as the story unfolds.

Newbie – a new writer who has not yet been published.

No, and Furthermore – a type of "disaster" ending when planning the Scene. The POV character does not achieve his Scene goal, and furthermore gains more problems. This is an effective type of Scene ending.

Noah's Ark – editing term describing presence of modifiers written two by two.

Obstacle – Internal and external problems that prevent the protagonist from achieving his goal.

Offset Printing – a common type of printing in which books are printed from plates. Normally a minimum of at least 500 books is necessary to make the run financially feasible. The other common method of printing is POD.

Old World – protagonist's environment before he moves into the challenge of the main story's new world.

Ordinary World – demonstrated in the first part of act one. Protagonist's world before the story starts, often with a sense of suffocation or slow death.

Orphan – The protagonist role in act one. Pearson expands on this topic.

PCN – Preassigned Control Number; a number received from the Library of Congress before a book's publication that uniquely identifies the book in its catalog.

PDF – Portable Document Format; computer file that retains formatting with images across forums. Can be used for an e-book format and read on e-readers or on computer using Adobe Acrobat.

Perfect Bound –common type of book binding for soft-cover books in which glue holds the book pages to the book spine. Paperback books are perfect bound.

Pitch –100-200 word description of the story that is written to intrigue.

Platform – personal following for an author or potential author; includes things like speaking engagements, articles, and internet presence. The platform is important for the author to promote his book title.

POD – Print on Demand; a type of printing in which books are produced one at a time. The other common method of printing is offset printing.

Point of View (POV) – in third person limited, the viewpoint from which the story is told. The reader has access to the character's thoughts and emotions as well as the outer events.

POV character – the character through whose eyes the scene is told.

Premise – fundamental concept that drives the story.

Preparation for Battle – first part of act three, in which the protagonist develops a crazy plan that is unlikely but could work against the antagonist. Protagonist and his friends prepare for confrontation with antagonist.

Print on Demand – see POD.

Protagonist – Main character about whom the story is about.

Protagonist Disintegrates – one of three themes of act two/part two, in which the protagonist after the midpoint continues to lose ground.

Protagonist's Mirror – a character that faces the same essential problem as the protagonist, but solves it in a different, usually worse, way. (Story Strand E).

Query Letter – a one page letter that intriguingly introduces a writer's manuscript to a literary agent or editor.

Recurring character – a character that is clearly identifiable and persistently present in the story. This character may be a main one or a bit one.

Resolution – last stage of the story. Shows how the world and protagonist will now go on after the protagonist has conquered the story goal and navigated his character arc.

Response – second part of motivation reaction unit (MRU), a re-action by the character that goes in the order of emotion or sensation, reflex action, rational action, and speech.

Reveal – shorthand notation that describes action progression. Set in the form "character goal → BUT an obstacle appears."

Romantic Interest – character that acts as object of protagonist's pursuit. Often this character sees the protagonist's core before anyone else.

Royalties – monies paid to an author from a traditional publisher as proportion of book sales, once book advance is paid back.

SASE – letter-sized self-addressed stamped envelope. This should accompany all correspondence to an agent or editor.

Scene – a unit with a goal, conflict, and disaster that mainly follows the external conflict.

Scene Conflict – main center part of scene that deals with multiple obstacles as POV character works to achieve scene goal.

Scene Goal – clearly articulated goal that the protagonist wishes to achieve in the scene.

Scene Disaster – ending part of scene that answers the scene goal question, and often ends with the POV character in a worse situation than before it started.

Self-Publish – author coordinates tasks to publish book under his own imprint. Often confused with Subsidy Publishing.

Sequel – a unit with emotion, thought, decision, and action, that describes the POV character's reaction to the previous Scene disaster.

Slide – last event of act two/part two; an often spectacular event that narrows protagonist's options so that the nature of the climax is now clearly seen. As Blake Snyder identified in *Save the Cat!*, there is usually a death of some sort (person, idea, place) in this scene.

Snail Mail – regular mail sent through the US Postal System or other country's postal system.

Sole Proprietorship – a type of company in which the individual simply creates a name and opens for business, without paperwork. For tax purposes and other legal matters, the sole proprietorship is treated like the individual.

Spoiler – revelation of plot twist in a synopsis or other story summary.

Stakes – what the protagonist and others may lose if they cannot achieve Story Goal.

Stimulus – first part of motivation reaction unit (MRU), an external prompt to the character that causes him to want to act.

Story Boarding – technique often used by screenwriters to plan out the story sequence.

Story Goal – the prize that the protagonist seeks during the course of the story. The attainment, or not, of this Story Goal is answered clearly and unambiguously at the end of the story.

Story Pillars – four general areas of story development (plot, character, moral, story world).

Story Post – story template markers that occur reliably within certain positions. (inciting, door, midpoint, slide, darkest moment, help from outside, climax, resolution).

Story Question – whether the protagonist will be able to achieve the story goal.

Story Strand – Story line type. Strands include A (main story), B (protagonist's hidden need), C (antagonist), D (gift at climax), and E (protagonist's mirror).

Story Template – the stable pattern of story structure.

Submission package – written materials that introduce your manuscript to a literary agent or editor. Items may include one-page query letter, short and long synopsis, book proposal including marketing plan, and highly polished first 25 pages (or first three chapters) of your manuscript.

Subplot – additional story line that reinforces themes, complicates the plot, and/or deepens character development.

Subsidy Publishing – type of publishing in which the author pays to have his book published.

Switch Away –a common beat occurring in act two/part one, usually right after the door. The Switch Away beat serves to break the story tension after the door by following a subplot line, usually the antagonist's (C story strand).

Synopsis – summary of a story in one or a few pages. This document allows other readers (editors, agents) to evaluate the story without having to read the entire manuscript.

Tension – the uncertainty of at least one issue in the story.

Theme Changes – contrast the old and new world. Some examples are present to past, alone to together, material to spiritual values, fear to faith, and so on.

Three Act Structure – traditional story structure first postulated by Aristotle.

Ticking Clock – A technique to raise story tension in which a time limit to accomplish a goal is introduced in the story.

Traditional Publishing – the publishing company pays to have the book published.

Wanderer – The protagonist role in act two/part one. Pearson expands on this topic.

Warrior –The protagonist role in act two/part two. Pearson expands on this topic.

Wound (protagonist wound) – an unhealed source of continuing pain occurring usually before the story begins or possibly the prologue. The wound is undeserved and can be from a single event or, more commonly, an extended situation.

Yes, But – a type of disaster ending when planning the Scene. The POV character achieves his Scene goal, but also gains more problems. This is an effective type of Scene ending.

Appendix One

How-To Writing Books
and Other Resources

So many excellent resources, so little time. In this list I give a few titles that may be particularly helpful for you. This list is not exhaustive, and my apologies to all those wonderful authors whom I didn't mention.

Bell, James Scott. *Write Great Fiction: Revision and Self-Editing*. 2008 (2nd ed.): Writer's Digest Books.

Published by *Writer's Digest*, this is part of a series on writing techniques. The first half of this book reviews techniques for fiction such as point of view. The second half gives remedies for problems such as boring dialogue and sagging middle. Lots of examples make his points clear. Highly recommended.

Bickham, Jack. *Elements of Fiction Writing: Scene and Structure*. 1999: Writer's Digest Books.

Published by *Writer's Digest*, this is part of a series on writing techniques. Bickham's lucid explanation of how to set up the scene and sequel generated that amazing "a-ha" moment for me. For that section alone, it's worth a look.

Browne, Renni, and King, David. *Self-Editing for Fiction Writers: How to Edit Yourself Into Print.* **1993, 2004: Harper Paperbacks.**

Editing is essential to make your pages shine. This book goes over many points you may not have thought of to improve your manuscript, such as handling exposition, improving pacing, and developing a "voice." Highly recommended.

Card, Orson Scott. *Elements of Fiction Writing: Characters and Viewpoint.* **1999: Writer's Digest Books.**

Published by *Writer's Digest*, this is part of a series on writing techniques. The light bulb flashed on for me while learning about techniques for deep character penetration in point of view. I didn't link till later that this author was the same who wrote *Ender's Game*, one of my three all-time favorite novels. Highly recommended.

Dixon, Debra. *Goal, Motivation, and Conflict: The Building Blocks of Good Fiction.* **1999: Gryphon Books for Writers.**

Dixon gives clear instruction for the smaller units of fiction development. The GMC is a critical concept if you want to write well enough to become published. This book can be purchased from the publisher at Gryphon books for Writers at http://www.gryphonbooksforwriters.com. Highly recommended.

Dunne, Will. *The Dramatic Writer's Companion: Tools to Develop Characters, Cause Scenes, and Build Stories.* **2009: University of Chicago Press.**

This insightful book puts forth questions to sharpen and refine your work. Dunne finishes with a practical troubleshooting guide to identify and repair bugaboos such as lacking conflict in a scene or a passive main character. Highly recommended for writer's block.

Field, Syd. *Screenplay: The Foundations of Screenwriting.* **2005 (revised): Delta.**

Field is a giant in the field of helping screenwriters learn their craft. This classic book gives a good foundation for the beginning writer. It tends to be heavy on rules, but as you become more experienced you can learn to flex and go beyond.

Frey, James. *How to Write a Damn Good Novel: A Step-by-Step No Nonsense Guide to Dramatic Storytelling.* **1987: St. Martin's Press.**

An excellent general discussion of the components of a good novel. Frey also gives a healthy dose of motivation, and writes in an entertaining and fun style.

Hauge, Michael and Vogler, Christopher. *The Hero's 2 Journeys: Insider Secrets for Uniting the Outer Journey of Plot Structure with the Inner Journey of Character Arc.* **2003: Writer's AudioShop.**

Two renowned screenwriting instructors give a seminar to discuss story structure. These DVDs take some time to watch, but are highly informative.

Ingermanson, Randy, and Economy, Peter. *Writing Fiction for Dummies.* **2009: For Dummies.**

Randy is my hero. Peter Economy is another professional writer, and together they have created something really helpful here. This book uses a number of Randy's writing techniques including his famous "Snowflake" to help you develop a writing routine, design and finish a novel, and create a book proposal and marketing plan. Here is inspiring and can-do advice especially for the newbie.

Kernen, Robert. *Building Better Plots.* **1999: Writer's Digest Books.**

Kernen deconstructs plots into elements such as inciting incident, rising action, character arcs and so forth, with lots of interactive charts and questions that help you put together a great story. Insightful, practical, and helpful.

Leal, Carmen. *You Can Market Your Book: All the Tools You Need to Sell Your Published Book.* **2003: ACW Press.**

There are many marketing books out there. This is a good one, even though it's a little older. I met Ms. Leal at a writer's conference, and ideas for marketing anything just flew out of her head. This book models that can-do and creative attitude.

Levine, Mark. *The Fine Print of Self-Publishing: Everything You Need to Know about the Costs, Contracts, and Process of Self-Publishing.* **2011 (4th ed.): Bascom Hill Publishing Group.**

Levine is an attorney who studied contracts from a selected group of subsidy publishers, and his findings and discussions can be generalized to many other companies. Levine discusses potential landmines that may exist and what you can expect from this type of publishing experience. If you are considering publishing your book yourself, and don't plan to form your own company to do so, you simply must read this book to protect yourself before entering into any sort of agreement. Highly recommended.

Larsen, Michael. *How to Write a Book Proposal*. 2011 (4th ed.): Writer's Digest Books.

This book is a classic, written by a literary agent who knows the publishing business. Written for nonfiction, but many of the ideas can also be transferred to fiction.

Lukeman, Noah. *The First Five Pages: A Writer's Guide to Stay Out of the Rejection Pile*. 2005: Fireside.

Lukeman is a successful literary agent who doesn't mince words as he describes what will send a manuscript to the reject pile before its potential may be evaluated. Comprised of tips for grammar, formatting, and presentation, this book includes exercises at the end of each chapter that will help you to eradicate manuscript red flags before sending out your words.

Lukeman, Noah. *How to Land (and Keep) a Literary Agent*. Available as an ebook in PDF format and for Amazon Kindle and Barnes&Noble Nook at http://www.lukeman.com/landaliteraryagent/**.**

This book covers the nuts and bolts of actually finding a literary agent, including resources for identifying suitable agents, how to approach and follow up contacts, and how to form a happy agent-author relationship. If you're ready to go through this process, you'll find this book indispensable.

Lukeman, Noah. *How to Write a Great Query Letter: Insider Tips and Techniques for Success.* **Available as an ebook in PDF format and for Amazon Kindle.**

Lukeman is a successful literary agent who has read thousands of query letters, and knows what makes them work. He offers this book for free in PDF and for Amazon Kindle at http://www.lukeman.com/greatquery/download.htm. The price is right.

Maass, Donald. *Writing the Breakout Novel* **(2002) and** *Writing the Breakout Novel Workbook* **(2004). Writer's Digest Books.**

Maass is a successful literary agent who has deeply studied books that have "broken out" and grab readers. He explains what works, and includes challenging and thoughtful exercises to do once you have finished your first draft. You will not finish your second draft for a long time, but it will become so strong you won't recognize it. Highly recommended.

McCutcheon, Pam. *Writing the Fiction Synopsis: A Step by Step Approach.* **1998: Gryphon Books for Writers.**

McCutcheon breaks down writing the synopsis and gives many examples that will help guide you to write something decent. This book is also helpful if you are simply trying to work out what your story is about. You can purchase from the publisher, Gryphon Books for Writers, at http://www.gryphonbooksforwriters.com. Highly recommended.

McGee, Robert. *Story: Substance, Structure, Style, and the Principles of Screenwriting.* **1997: It Books.**

A classic in screenwriting, McGee gives principles to constructing great scenes and compelling characters. Highly recommended for both novelists and screenwriters.

Noble, William. *Elements of Fiction Writing: Conflict, Action, and Suspense.* **1999: Writer's Digest Books.**

Published by *Writer's Digest,* this is part of a series on writing techniques. Noble's techniques for creating drama (emotional involvement, immediacy, escalating the stakes) may seem formulaic, but he has good points. This book is helpful for anyone starting out.

Pearson, Carol S. The *Hero Within: Six Archetypes We Live By.* **1998: Harper One.**

This is not a writing book, but an insightful examination of common life roles and moving toward living out the positive characteristics of the hero. A good complement to Campbell's and Vogler's work with the hero's journey.

Rosenthal, Morris. *Print-On-Demand Book Publishing: A New Approach to Printing and Marketing Books for Publishers and Self-Publishing Authors.* **2008: Foner Books.**

A nuts and bolts guide to preparing and distributing your self-published book using POD (print on demand) technology. No information on e-books.

Scofield, Sandra. *The Scene Book: A Primer for the Fiction Writer.* **2007: Penguin.**

Scofield looks at a unit of story construction: the scene, and discusses how to focus so that it resonates. Step by step instructions, examples, and exercises guide to write something effective. Very helpful.

Shepard, Aaron. *Perfect Pages: Self Publishing with Microsoft Word, or How to Design Your Own Book for Desktop Publishing and Print on Demand.* **2006: Shepard Publications.**

Typesetting, or designing text for a book, is not as easy as it looks. While specialized programs give a more beautiful and professional design, it is possible to typeset using Word. This book shows you how.

Snyder, Blake. *Save the Cat!* **(2005) and** *Save the Cat! Strikes Back* **(2009). Michael Wiese Productions.**

Snyder was a successful Hollywood screenwriter who sadly died in August 2009. He starts with a 15 point story progression, then breaks it out into 40 beats (bubbles in my vernacular) that are ready to write for the screenplay. *Save the Cat!* is perhaps my favorite book about story structure (I go between this one and Truby's *The Anatomy of Story*). *Save the Cat! Strikes Back* gives a general compilation of hints for story and career that are truly insightful. Both books highly recommended.

Swain, Dwight. *Techniques of the Selling Writer.* **1982 (first published 1965): University of Oklahoma Press.**

A bit impervious for my taste, somewhat dated, but Swain solidly covers elements of fiction writing and gives meticulous reviews of techniques. My favorite discussions center on the importance of "small" structure (motivation-reaction units) and the emotional bonding of the reader with the characters. This is a classic.

Trottier, David. *The Screenwriter's Bible: A Complete Guide to Writing, Formatting, and Selling Your Script.* **2010 (5th ed.): Silman-James Press.**

The name says it all. Comprehensive, well-written, and good information.

Truby, John. *The Anatomy of Story: 22 Steps to Becoming a Master Storyteller*. 2008: Faber & Faber.

You'll need to work through this intellectual book slowly with your story development notebook in the other hand. Truby sticks with the essential through line of the story, and especially the all-important changes that must occur in the protagonist to make the story gripping and resonant. I love this book. Highly recommended.

Vogler, Christopher. *The Writer's Journey: Mythic Structures for Writers*. 2007 (3rd ed.): Michael Wiese Productions.

Based on Joseph Campbell's academic 1949 work *The Hero with a Thousand Faces*, Vogler explores the common mythological elements present in all stories. This scholarly book isn't as accessible as some, but is a classic that offers excellent help and insight into the story structure.

Whalin, W. Terry. *Book Proposals that Sell: 21 Secrets to Speed Your Success*. 2005: Write Now Publications.

Having been both an editor and a literary agent, Whalin has insider information for how you can present your book with the specifics that will gain notice when you're ready to find a publisher. While this book is written for nonfiction, much crosses into fiction proposals. Lots of website resources, examples, and specifics. Christian perspective.

Appendix Two

Sample Synopses

Dracula

An unlikely group of professionals and friends discovers a mythical evil that is surprisingly real and determined to infiltrate 1900s England.

A young English lawyer, JONATHAN HARKER, travels to Transylvania to meet with a client of his firm, COUNT DRACULA. Dracula wishes to purchase real estate in England. As Harker travels through the exotic countryside by coach, the local people become alarmed whenever they learn of his destination. A peasant woman hangs a crucifix around his neck for protection from what Harker learns they call the "vampire."

Uneasily Harker reaches his coach ride's last destination point to meet the count's carriage. The driver says not a word, but when mysterious blue lights appear several times on the plain the driver stops and exits for a few minutes. Wolves nearly attack, and the journey seems endless. However, once Harker arrives he finds Dracula intelligent and well-educated. Dinner and a charming apartment invitingly wait.

After a few days, though, Harker realizes that he is in reality a prisoner in the castle. The count has no reflection in the mirror, and climbs walls like a bat. A sense of evil pervades the castle. One night Harker falls asleep and encounters three dream-like females whom the count chases away, saying that he needs Harker for a little longer. Fearing for his life, Harker attempts to escape from the castle by climbing down the outside walls, but cannot. He fears he will go mad.

Back in England, Harker's fiancée MINA MURRAY has been writing to her best friend, LUCY WESTENRA. Lucy has received marriage proposals from three men in one day—DR. JOHN SEWARD, ARTHUR HOLMWOOD, and a Texan named QUINCEY MORRIS. She is sad to have to hurt two of the men, but accepts Holmwood's proposal.

Mina visits Lucy at the seaside town of Whitby. A Russian ship wrecks on the shore, carrying a cargo of fifty boxes of earth shipped from Castle Dracula. No one is on board except a large dog that bounds ashore and disappears. Soon after, Mina becomes concerned as Lucy begins sleepwalking, and follows her into the cemetery where a dark shape with glowing red eyes bends over Lucy. In the following days Lucy becomes pale and ill, with two tiny red marks at her throat that Mina believes she caused when she pinned a cape on her that night. Dr. Seward cannot diagnose Lucy's illness, so he sends for his old teacher PROFESSOR VAN HELSING.

Soon after, Mina learns that her fiancé Jonathan is suffering from brain fever in the city of Budapest, and goes to join him. Van Helsing arrives to Whitby, examines Lucy, then orders for her room to be filled with garlic, a defense against vampires. Lucy sleeps several nights in peace until her mother opens the windows and removes the garlic. Lucy is found the next morning pale and weak.

Seward and Van Helsing work over Lucy for several days and give her blood transfusions from each of the three men who proposed to her, plus Van Helsing. At night when Lucy's mother opens the window, a large dog appears at the window and scares the mother to death, then attacks Lucy. She is found dead.

A series of unexplained attacks on children by a "bloofer lady" begin. Van Helsing brings Holmwood, Seward, and Morris to Lucy's tomb to convince them that Lucy now is "Un-Dead"—a vampire perpetrating these attacks. The men remain skeptical until they see Lucy prey upon a child. This convinces them that she must be destroyed. The next morning, Holmwood acting as Lucy's husband stakes her through the heart. The men then cut off her head and stuff her mouth with garlic. Although they have performed a grisly task, the men are content they have ushered Lucy into eternal rest.

Mina and Jonathan, now married, return to England and are shocked by the turn of events. Mina collates diary and journal entries of her husband and the other men to discover clues of Count Dracula. The group tracks down forty-nine of the fifty boxes of earth that the count must sleep in when away from his castle, and sterilizes them with holy wafer.

One of Dr. Seward's mental patients, R.M. RENFIELD, has some interaction with the count and invites him into the asylum where the group is staying. This allows the count to begin to prey upon Mina.

Mina exhibits the same symptoms as Lucy as she slowly begins changing into a vampire. Since the count has lost his boxes of earth he is no longer safe in England so flees to the safety of his native Transylvania. The group splits up to pursue the count. Mina goes with Van Helsing. In the castle the group destroys the three women vampires and seals the area with holy objects. As the count arrives to the castle, the group attacks and overcomes him. Morris is killed in the crossfire. The group is exhausted but satisfied that they have rid the world of a great evil.

The Count of Monte Cristo

A wrongfully-imprisoned young man gains freedom and a fortune that he uses to wreak an elaborate revenge.

This story takes place in the grand sweep of Napoleonic France. Nineteen-year-old sailor EDMOND DANTÈS has just been promoted to ship's captain, and plans to marry his great love MERCÉDÈS in a few days. Unfortunately, dangerous jealousy stirs the hearts of three of his so-called friends. DANGLARS, the ship's treasurer, wishes for Edmond's promotion himself. FERNAND MONDEGO is in love with Mercédès. GASPARD CADEROUSSE is a hanger-on and drunk who simply covets Edmond's charmed life.

As a joke the three men write a letter accusing Edmond of treason, but then cruelly go ahead to post it. Because Edmond, on the dying order of his captain, carries a letter from Napoleon to an ardent Bonapartist in Paris, there is evidence to convict him although Edmond himself has no political interest. During his wedding feast, right before the marriage ceremony, Edmond is arrested.

The deputy public prosecutor GÉRARD DE VILLEFORT finds Edmond to be a pleasant and candid youth with no political leanings. He prepares to release him until Edmond mentions the name of the person to receive Napoleon's letter: NOIRTIER DE VILLEFORT. Villefort is terrified because Noitier is Villefort's estranged father, and release of his name would jeopardize Villefort's political standing and career. Villefort decides to send Edmond to prison for life so that he cannot tell anyone about Noitier. Edmond's kind and honest boss, PIERRE MORREL, repeatedly begs for Edmond's release to no avail. Edmond is imprisoned in the impregnable prison for dangerous political prisoners, the Château D'If.

Edmond is locked in a solitary rock room for years, and almost goes mad from isolation until he meets a fellow prisoner tunneling under his cell. The ABBÉ FARIA is an Italian priest and intellectual who was jailed for his political views. Faria educates Edmond in history, philosophy, science, and languages. However when Faria tells Edmond about an unimaginable treasure Edmond worries his friend is insane. Soon after Faria dies, and Edmond sews himself in Faria's shroud thinking he'll be able to dig himself out of a grave. Instead Edmond is thrown into the sea, and barely able to cut himself loose. He swims to freedom.

Edmond travels to the isolated island of Monte Cristo to find Faria's treasure, and realizes he will be able to righteously take revenge on those who behaved so evilly to him. Disguising himself as ABBÉ BUSONI, an Italian priest, he travels to Marseilles to find Caderousse. Caderousse tells the abbé that Edmond's father died of starvation, Mercédès married Fernand, and both Danglars and Fernand are now rich and powerful. Edmond gives Caderousse a precious diamond, saying that Edmond had bequeathed it to Fernand, Danglars, and Caderousse, and Caderousse was obviously the only one who had been loyal.

In Marseilles Edmond also learns about his previous boss Morrel's repeated efforts to free him from prison, and anonymously saves him from financial ruin.

Ten years later Edmond calls himself the Count of Monte Cristo, and uses his wealth and power to form a glittering disguise. In Rome he engineers the rescuing of Fernand's and Mercédès' son ALBERT DE MORCERF so that Albert will introduce him to Parisian society. Edmond thus can naturally interact with Danglars, Fernand, and Villefort. He has spent the previous ten years gathering information to enact elaborate revenges against each of them.

Villefort's house is troubled, and Edmond discovers its secrets. First he seemingly innocently gives knowledge of poisons to Villefort's wife, since she wants to advance her son over Villefort's daughter VALENTINE from a previous marriage. Edmond is content to let all of Villefort's house die from poison until he learns that the son of his boss, MAXIMILIEN MORREL, has fallen in love with Valentine. In an elaborate scheme he saves her and brings them together.

Once Villefort discovers the guilt of his wife he gives her a choice of suicide or public prosecution; she kills herself and her son. Edmond then exposes a scandal in which Villefort killed his illegitimate baby son (although the baby was rescued, Villefort didn't know this). Since everyone in his family is dead, and he will be publicly prosecuted, Villefort goes insane.

Although Fernand had grown up undistinguished, he now has an enormous fortune and has become the Count de Morcerf. Edmond searched and found the daughter of Greek vizier ALI PACHA, whom Fernand had betrayed when she was a child in order to make his fortune. Fernand robbed Ali Pacha's fortune and sold the woman, HAYDÉE, and her mother into slavery. Haydée testifies against Fernand in front of the senate, publicly and irreversibly humiliating him and destroying the honor of the entire family. Albert and Mercédès run away, and Fernand commits suicide.

For his revenge on Danglars, Edmond bankrupts him and facilitates Danglars' daughter to run away. Finally Edmond arranges for Danglars to be kidnapped to drain every last penny from him, then shows him mercy by releasing him with his life.

After his God-like repayment of deeds has been accomplished, Edmond feels empty. He is surprised and delighted to learn that Haydée has fallen in love with him, since he is in love with her but never wished to behave dishonorably by making his feelings known. He and Haydée sail together into the sunset.

In this book Edmond discovers the dark side of revenge, and learns that forgiveness ultimately frees the soul.

Appendix Three

Examples of Opening Lines

Here are some of the best opening lines of novels as selected by editors from *American Book Review*.

"Call me Ishmael." —Herman Melville, *Moby-Dick* (1851)

"It is a truth universally acknowledged, that a single man in possession of a good fortune, must be in want of a wife." —Jane Austen, *Pride and Prejudice* (1813)

"Many years later, as he faced the firing squad, Colonel Aureliano Buendía was to remember that distant afternoon when his father took him to discover ice." —Gabriel García Márquez, *One Hundred Years of Solitude* (1967; trans. Gregory Rabassa)

"It was a bright cold day in April, and the clocks were striking thirteen." —George Orwell, *1984* (1949)

"I am an invisible man." —Ralph Ellison, *Invisible Man* (1952)

"Someone must have slandered Josef K., for one morning, without having done anything truly wrong, he was arrested." —Franz Kafka, *The Trial* (1925; trans. Breon Mitchell)

"The sun shone, having no alternative, on the nothing new." —Samuel Beckett, *Murphy* (1938)

"This is the saddest story I have ever heard." —Ford Madox Ford, *The Good Soldier* (1915)

"Whether I shall turn out to be the hero of my own life, or whether that station will be held by anybody else, these pages must show." —Charles Dickens, *David Copperfield* (1850)

"One summer afternoon Mrs. Oedipa Maas came home from a Tupperware party whose hostess had put perhaps too much kirsch in the fondue to find that she, Oedipa, had been named executor, or she supposed executrix, of the estate of one Pierce Inverarity, a California real estate mogul who had once lost two million dollars in his spare time but still had assets numerous and tangled enough to make the job of sorting it all out more than honorary." —Thomas Pynchon, *The Crying of Lot 49* (1966)

"It was a wrong number that started it, the telephone ringing three times in the dead of night, and the voice on the other end asking for someone he was not." —Paul Auster, *City of Glass* (1985)

"124 was spiteful." —Toni Morrison, *Beloved* (1987)

"Mother died today." —Albert Camus, *The Stranger* (1942; trans. Stuart Gilbert)

"Every summer Lin Kong returned to Goose Village to divorce his wife, Shuyu." - Ha Jin, *Waiting* (1999)

"Once an angry man dragged his father along the ground through his own orchard. 'Stop!' cried the groaning old man at last, 'Stop! I did not drag my father beyond this tree.'" —Gertrude Stein, *The Making of Americans* (1925)

"Mrs. Dalloway said she would buy the flowers herself." —Virginia Woolf, *Mrs. Dalloway* (1925)

"All this happened, more or less." —Kurt Vonnegut, *Slaughterhouse-Five* (1969)

"They shoot the white girl first." —Toni Morrison, *Paradise* (1998)

"The moment one learns English, complications set in." —Felipe Alfau, *Chromos* (1990)

"I had the story, bit by bit, from various people, and, as generally happens in such cases, each time it was a different story." —Edith Wharton, *Ethan Frome* (1911)

"There was a boy called Eustace Clarence Scrubb, and he almost deserved it." —C. S. Lewis, *The Voyage of the Dawn Treader* (1952)

"It was the day my grandmother exploded." —Iain M. Banks, *The Crow Road* (1992)

"It was a pleasure to burn." —Ray Bradbury, *Fahrenheit 451* (1953)

"In the beginning, sometimes I left messages in the street." — David Markson, *Wittgenstein's Mistress* (1988)

"It was love at first sight." —Joseph Heller, *Catch-22* (1961)

"Once upon a time, there was a woman who discovered she had turned into the wrong person." —Anne Tyler, *Back When We Were Grownups* (2001)

"In my younger and more vulnerable years my father gave me some advice that I've been turning over in my mind ever since." —F. Scott Fitzgerald, *The Great Gatsby* (1925)

"You better not never tell nobody but God." —Alice Walker, The Color Purple (1982)

"'To be born again,' sang Gibreel Farishta tumbling from the heavens, 'first you have to die.'" —Salman Rushdie, *The Satanic Verses* (1988)

"It was a queer, sultry summer, the summer they electrocuted the Rosenbergs, and I didn't know what I was doing in New York." —Sylvia Plath, *The Bell Jar* (1963)

"If I am out of my mind, it's all right with me, thought Moses Herzog." —Saul Bellow, *Herzog* (1964)

"Francis Marion Tarwater's uncle had been dead for only half a day when the boy got too drunk to finish digging his grave and a Negro named Buford Munson, who had come to get a jug filled, had to finish it and drag the body from the breakfast table where it was still sitting and bury it in a decent and Christian way, with the sign of its Saviour at the head of the grave and enough dirt on top to keep the dogs from digging it up." —Flannery O'Connor, *The Violent Bear it Away* (1960)

"When Dick Gibson was a little boy he was not Dick Gibson." —Stanley Elkin, *The Dick Gibson Show* (1971)

"Hiram Clegg, together with his wife Emma and four friends of the faith from Randolph Junction, were summoned by the Spirit and Mrs. Clara Collins, widow of the beloved Nazarene preacher Ely Collins, to West Condon on the weekend of the eighteenth and nineteenth of April, there to await the End of the World." —Robert Coover, *The Origin of the Brunists* (1966)

"'Take my camel, dear,' said my Aunt Dot, as she climbed down from this animal on her return from High Mass." —Rose Macaulay, *The Towers of Trebizond* (1956)

"The past is a foreign country; they do things differently there."
—L. P. Hartley, *The Go-Between* (1953)

"Justice? - You get justice in the next world, in this world you have the law." —William Gaddis, *A Frolic of His Own* (1994)

"Vaughan died yesterday in his last car-crash." —J. G. Ballard, *Crash* (1973)

"I write this sitting in the kitchen sink." —Dodie Smith, *I Capture the Castle* (1948)

"'When your mama was the geek, my dreamlets,' Papa would say, 'she made the nipping off of noggins such a crystal mystery that the hens themselves yearned toward her, waltzing around her, hypnotized with longing.'" —Katherine Dunn, *Geek Love* (1983)

"When I finally caught up with Abraham Trahearne, he was drinking beer with an alcoholic bulldog named Fireball Roberts in a ramshackle joint just outside of Sonoma, California, drinking the heart right out of a fine spring afternoon." —James Crumley, *The Last Good Kiss* (1978)

"It was just noon that Sunday morning when the sheriff reached the jail with Lucas Beauchamp though the whole town (the whole county too for that matter) had known since the night before that Lucas had killed a white man." —William Faulkner, *Intruder in the Dust* (1948)

"I, Tiberius Claudius Drusus Nero Germanicus This-that-and-the-other (for I shall not trouble you yet with all my titles) who was once, and not so long ago either, known to my friends and relatives and associates as 'Claudius the Idiot,' or 'That Claudius,' or 'Claudius the Stammerer,' or 'Clau-Clau-Claudius' or at best as 'Poor Uncle Claudius,' am now about to write this strange history of my life; starting from my earliest childhood and continuing year by year until I reach the fateful point of change where, some eight years ago, at the age of fifty-one, I suddenly found myself caught in what I may call the 'golden predicament' from which I have never since become disentangled." —Robert Graves, *I, Claudius* (1934)

"Of all the things that drive men to sea, the most common disaster, I've come to learn, is women." —Charles Johnson, *Middle Passage* (1990)

"He was born with a gift of laughter and a sense that the world was mad." —Raphael Sabatini, *Scaramouche* (1921)

"Psychics can see the color of time it's blue." —Ronald Sukenick, *Blown Away* (1986)

"In the town, there were two mutes and they were always together." —Carson McCullers, *The Heart is a Lonely Hunter* (1940)

"Time is not a line but a dimension, like the dimensions of space." —Margaret Atwood, *Cat's Eye* (1988)

"High, high above the North Pole, on the first day of 1969, two professors of English Literature approached each other at a combined velocity of 1200 miles per hour." —David Lodge, *Changing Places* (1975)

Appendix Four

Sample Edit

Below, I've included a sample before-and-after-editing passage from my novel, *A Lever Long Enough*. I face off the draft and final versions section by section, and after each section give a brief explanation for the changes I made. The draft passage is 382 words, the final is 329. This gives a word reduction of fourteen percent.

My book is about a small military team that travels back in time to film the theft of Jesus' body from the tomb. It isn't religious, although obviously it touches upon religious themes. It is respectful of Christianity. In this excerpt, my protagonist Benjamin is trapped in a first century house with a native whom he doesn't trust. Benjamin also has a wounded man with him. The chapter begins as another man enters the dwelling.

DRAFT: (108 words)

The door opened from the narrow street into the first century house. The man was tall and bearded, and he loomed as a dark shape blocking the late afternoon light. Benjamin leaned protectively over the unconscious David who lay in the shadow of the room's platform at the back of the room. He didn't think they were immediately visible from the street.

"What is this?" the man demanded.

Benjamin was aware of being in great danger from this older man with the physician's stripe on his robe who could turn them into the Roman authorities. The man was glaring at Eleazar suspiciously.

"What is what, Uncle?" Eleazar asked.

FINAL: (78 words)

Benjamin leaned protectively over the unconscious David as the door opened from the narrow street into the first century house. David lay in the shadow of the platform at the back of the room, and Benjamin didn't think he was immediately visible from the street. The man pushing open the door was tall and bearded, and he loomed as a dark shape blocking the light.

"What is this?" the man demanded, glaring at Eleazar.

"What is what, Uncle?"

NOTES:

POV in draft is not clear from chapter first line. Some extraneous words and speaker attributions cut.

DRAFT: *(156 words)*

Benjamin furrowed his brow as he glanced again at David's bruised face, streaked on the right side with dried blood from the head wound. Yet he was wary of Eleazar too, an unknown who seemed to be choreographing events even as he watched everything from the back of the room. Cloaked motives of that one. Yet they had no choice.

"There is blood to my door," the older man said. "Small drops. I followed it all along the street, and now you're here. What does it mean?"

"Blood," Benjamin murmured, and he felt himself turn pale. The man turned suddenly to him, and then he gasped as his gaze slid for the first time to David in the shadows. He reached down and picked up one of the bloody cloths that had fallen to the floor.

A trail of blood. But the Romans would have found them now if they were going to. Wouldn't they have?

FINAL: *(141 words)*

Benjamin furrowed his brow as he glanced again at David's bruised face, streaked on the right side with dried blood from the head wound. He was wary of Eleazar too, an unknown who seemed to be choreographing events even as he watched everything from the back of the room.

"There is blood leading to my door," the older man said. "Not much, but enough. I followed it all along the street, and find you're here. What does it mean?"

"Blood." Benjamin felt himself turn pale. The man whipped around to him, and then he gasped as his gaze caught David in the shadows. He reached down and picked up one of the bloody cloths that had fallen to the floor.

A trail of blood. But the Romans would have found them by now if they were trying to. Wouldn't they have?

NOTES:

Draft has extraneous thoughts and speech tags. "Turned suddenly" is replaced by the stronger verb "whipped." "Slid for the first time" is replaced by "caught."

DRAFT: (118 words)

He whispered desperately into the microphone on his wristband. Silence. He still was unable to establish contact with Sara or Rebecca.

"What happened to him?" the man demanded quickly of Benjamin. He pulled off his overcoat and flung it onto the platform next to Eleazar. "I am Matthias, a physician, as my nephew must have told you. Maybe I can help." He dropped smoothly to his knees next to David.

The room was semi-dark, lit only by the late sunlight streaming through the door and the two narrow, slit-light windows. After a moment Matthias made a disgusted noise – "Tcha" – and began to pull at the mat David was lying upon.

"Let's move him into the light," he said. "Help me."

FINAL: (110 words)

Desperate, he pressed the button on his wristband again, but there was only silence back. He still was unable to establish contact with Sara or Rebecca.

"What happened to him?" the man demanded of Benjamin.

He pulled off his overcoat and flung it next to Eleazar. "I am Matthias, as my nephew must have told you. Maybe I can help." He dropped to his knees beside David.

The room was semi-dark, the late sunlight streaming through both the door and the narrow window slits. After a moment, Matthias made a disgusted noise— "Tcha"—and pulled at the mat upon which David lay.

"Let's move him into the light. Help me."

NOTES:

The draft loses its adverbs and passive voice. Matthias has also lost his physician status.

These are small changes, but they make a big difference, don't you think?

Appendix Five

Self-Publishing Resources

With the advent of e-readers and e-books, and the easy accessibility of self-publishing resources, the publishing industry is in flux. Traditional publishers have strong resources for marketing a book. However, if you have a good platform and/ or only a small or well-focused group to whom you wish to make your book available, you may want to consider self-publishing.

Before starting, be cautious. Many people I know decide to self publish because they cannot gain the interest of an agent, but inability to find an agent is an important red flag. First, query enough literary agents to make sure that your book indeed can't find a home. Noah Lukeman, a literary agent who has written extensively about this process, advises in *How to Land (and Keep) a Literary Agent* that you may need to query fifty or more agents before finding one to accept your work.

If no one accepts your work, before spending time and money self-publishing consider carefully that you may have a problem with your book. The most common problem is that your writing is not yet up to "publishable" standards. Be brutally honest with yourself and keep working to improve your craft. Get as much feedback as you can.

Occasionally no agent will sign your manuscript, even if well written, because it isn't considered to be broadly saleable. Depending on your goals and realistic outlook, self-publishing may be a good choice in these circumstances.

There are four general types of publishing:

1. Traditional Publishing. This type of publishing is what most people think of, with houses such as Random House or Harper Collins. Literary agents work with traditional publishers. I discussed traditional publishing in Chapter Seventeen.

2. Subsidy and Print on Demand Publishing. In this type of publishing you pay a company to produce and distribute your work. A full-service print on demand company I feel I can recommend is YAV Publications (http://authors.interestingwriting.com/). There are other good ones also. Amazon's Create Space is largely do-it-yourself with reasonable printing costs (https://www.createspace.com/). Be cautious, though, because subsidy companies may partially or fully control pricing, rights, and distribution of your book as per the contract you sign with them. Read Mark Levine's book, *The Fine Print of Self-Publishing*, before you do anything else.

3. Self Publishing. You create a company, then outsource or do all the tasks necessary to produce and distribute a hard copy book made of paper and with a cover, as opposed to an e-book.

4. E-Publishing. If you have the rights to your book, you can e-publish this as an additional or sole outlet for your book sales. You don't need a company or ISBN to do this, although it's recommended. ISBN discussed below.

Self Publishing

Before you go ahead, develop a strong marketing plan to sell books. Once your book comes out, you'll be ready.

You need to form your own company, either a sole proprietorship or LLC. Although it's a little more work, I suggest for tax purposes and to protect your private assets that you consider establishing an LLC.

Strive to get endorsements for your book. Be creative—don't only think of well-known authors, but go to friends, fellow writers, and anyone who has a few letters after his name.

Write a sparkling back-cover copy and brief biography. Get a good-looking author photograph and a logo for your company.

To publish a book you need an ISBN, a cover PDF, and an interior PDF. You may also want to take a few extra steps to enable public libraries to easily categorize your book.

ISBNs (International Standard Book Number)

The ISBN is a unique identifier that forever is linked with your book. The ISBN is necessary to engage in generalized commerce in bookstores, online, and other venues—in other words, you can sell a book by hand without an ISBN, say a cookbook at a community function, but your opportunities without an ISBN are limited.

When self-publishing you want to purchase the ISBN directly from the official company in your global region. In the

USA this is Bowker Agency at http://www.bowker.com. If you purchase an ISBN from any other source, no matter what that source tells you the ISBN and your book will be linked to the source and not to you. I recommend purchasing a block of 10 ISBNs rather than one. Not only are the single ISBNs identifiable as singles and therefore for self-published books, but if you wish to release e-book versions you will need a different ISBN for each format.

Pick up any book on your shelf. On the back cover you should see a white box with two bar codes and also several strings of numbers. The larger barcode on the left encodes the book's ISBN, a thirteen digit number beginning with "978" if it's published in the USA. Since the system switched from ten to thirteen digits on January 1, 2007, the book may also have a ten digit ISBN. The smaller barcode on the right encodes the book's price in a five digit number. The number *90000* indicates no price specified.

Preparation for Public Libraries

An important and often overlooked market for books is public libraries, and you need to prepare for this market before publication.

This market requires a Library of Congress Control Number (LCCN). An LCCN is a unique identification number for your book in the Library of Congress' catalog record. Since you'll be applying before publication you need to get a Preassigned Control Number (PCN) (http://pcn.loc.gov/). The PCN requires cataloguing in publication (CIP) data, so you will also need to get your book data, called publisher-generated CIP data. The librarian I chose gave me a good price and fast turnaround of a few days at http://www.cipblock.com. There are other people who do this also; you can compare prices etc. with a google search. The CIP data allows individual libraries to categorize your book for their own shelves.

If you obtain a PCN, you will need to send a copy of your final book to the Library of Congress once it's published.

Cover PDF

The cover PDF consists of a cover image plus the cover design (front cover, back cover, and spine). You can do this yourself if you are meticulous, or hire someone to create and format this for you. Book covers are critical, so don't skimp.

Self-published titles often have a typical look that includes a generic-looking image on the front and a back cover with lots of space and a simple summary of the book or even just a short quote. You don't want this. You want your cover to look professional, so study traditionally-published covers and take time to develop yours with an attractive and unique front image, back cover summary, an endorsement or two, an author photo/bio, and company logo.

Many self publishers modify photos or images for their front covers. If you employ an image that isn't yours, carefully investigate rights and how you are permitted to modify and use it. Some web sites with stock photos available for free or low cost include:

www.istockphoto.com
www.photobucket.com
www.photoshopsupport.com/resources/stock-photos.html
www.sxc.hu
www.freedigitalphotos.net

www.freefoto.com

www.pdfphoto.org

www.search.creativecommons.org

www.clipart.com/en/

Interior PDF

The interior PDF arranges all the pages of a book into a PDF file. It includes the front matter, back matter, and book text. Front matter includes things like the title page, table of contents, copyright page, and acknowledgments page. Back matter may not be present or may include things such as an index or author's notes. Book text includes not just textual layout but running headers and page numbers, chapter headings, and other items such as section divider symbols. Study professionally designed books to learn layout requirements.

You can typeset your book yourself or hire it out. Typesetting is more complicated than it might seem, but it's doable if you have an artistic bent. Aaron Shepard in his book *Perfect Pages* reviews typesetting with Word to give a functional interior. There are also computer programs such as QuarkXpress and InDesign that do a much better job at typesetting. Again, it depends on how much you're willing to do and to spend. If you do typeset yourself, study professionally published books to find ideas to make yours look nice.

Printing

There are two major technologies for printing the softcover, perfect-bound book: POD (print on demand), and offset. POD technology can be thought of as a glorified copy machine in which books are printed one at a time. Offset printing technology uses plates to print a number of books at once, typically at least five-hundred or one thousand. For the reader holding the final product POD books are indistinguishable from offset printed books.

I recommend printing your books using POD technology since you won't have an inventory to store, although POD books are more expensive per unit. Offset printing requires a large outlay of cash to print the run and a storage facility for many books that may be harder to sell than you anticipate.

If you go POD, many small publishers use Lightning Source in LaVergne TN (http://wwww.lightningsource.com) as their printer. There are other printing companies also. Compare prices, quality, and customer service. As a self-publisher you can contract to use as many printers as you want, so if you're not happy the decision isn't irrevocable.

Resources

Self-Publishing is a complex area. I recommend you visit the following websites for the most up-to-date information:

Ron Pramschufer at http://www.publishingbasics.com/

Dan Poynter at http://www.parapublishing.com/

John Kremer at http://www.bookmarket.com/

Morris Rosenthal at http://www.fonerbooks.com/cornered.htm. He has also written a helpful book entitled *Print-on-Demand Book Publishing*.

E-Publishing

E-Publishing is turning traditional publishing on its head. An author can publish his book for free or low cost from his dining room table, and the easy availability of e-readers makes it likely people will purchase it. Traditional publishers are also eager to e-publish their books.

There are three basic formats for e-books:

1. PDF (portable document format).
2. .mobi format for Amazon's Kindle e-reader.
3. .ePub format for Barnes & Noble's Nook e-reader, Sony e-reader, and most or all other e-reader types except Amazon's Kindle.

PDF Format

PDFs are files that incorporate text and images in a fixed form. E-readers and computers read these files. The advantage for PDF format is these files represent exactly the formatting and appearance that the author builds in. The disadvantage for e-readers is these files are inflexible to manipulate for viewing and therefore may be less desirable than other formats.

To create a PDF from your Word or other file, simply use a PDF converter program. You can google free ones to download. A popular one is PrimoPDF at http://www.primopdf.com/download.aspx. To read a PDF on your computer, you will need to download a free copy of the application Adobe Acrobat if you don't already have this. This application can be found at http://get.adobe.com/reader/.

.mobi Format

The HTML-based .mobi format, and similar .azw format, are used for e-book documents for Amazon's Kindle e-reader. While you may wish to hire a professional to encode your document, there are also platforms that allow you to convert a Word document with images without knowing HTML.

To convert your Word document into a .mobi file using a

converter program, the document must have minimal formatting and no hard tabs. Put a page break after each chapter. Charts etc. must be imported as jpegs rather than formatted within the document. After creating an account, you can upload the Word document on the Amazon site at https://kdp.amazon.com/self-publishing/signin. Alternatively, you can convert your Word document through programs such as Scrivener (http://www.literatureandlatte.com/) or Calibre (http://calibre-ebook.com/), then upload the .mobi file onto the Amazon site. Verify the document looks correct through the preview window on amazon before publishing. If you find it isn't correct once you've published it, no worries. Simply make your changes, and re-upload.

.ePub Format

.ePub is considered the default e-reader format, and is also HTML-based. Just like the .mobi format, you can hire someone to convert your document or do it yourself. Barnes and Noble has a platform for the Nook to convert a minimally-formatted Word document with images at http://pubit.barnesandnoble.com/pubit_app/bn?t=pi_reg_home. Scrivener and Calibre convert documents into .ePub format. Do a Google search for other e-reader platforms, such as Sony, to upload your ebook.